A-Z STRATFORD-UPON-AVON, WARWICK & ROYAL LEAMINGTON SPA

C000256929

Stratford-upon-Avon, Henley-in-Arden, Warwick, Royal Leamington Spa, Whitnash, Barford, Bishop's Tachbrook, Hatton, Hampton Magna, Sherbourne, Longbridge, Snitterfield, Wilmcote, Alveston, Tiddington, Bridge Town, Clifford Chambers

Large Scale Town Centre 2 3

Reference

Motorway	M40
A Road	A46
B Road	B4632
Dual Carriageway	
One Way Street Traffic flow on A roads is indicated by a heavy line on the driver's left. All one way streets are shown on Large Scale Pages 2 & 3	
Pedestrianized Road	
Restricted Access	
Track & Footpath	
Railway (Level Crossing, Station)	
Built Up Area	CEDAR CL.
Local Authority Boundary	
Postcode Boundary	
Map Continuation	4 / Large Scale Town Centre 2
Car Park	P
Church or Chapel	†
Fire Station	■
Hospital	H
House Numbers A & B Roads only	22 48
Information Centre	i
National Grid Reference	420
Police Station	▲
Post Box Large Scale only	
Post Office	★
Public Telephone Large Scale only	
Toilet with facilities for the Disabled	
Viewpoint	
Educational Establishment	
Hospital or Health Centre	
Industrial Building	
Leisure or Recreational Facility	
Place of Interest	
Public Building	
Shopping Centre or Market	
Other Selected Buildings	

Scale

Pages 4-35
1:15,840 4 inches (10.16cm) to 1 mile 6.31cm to 1km
0 ¼ ½ Mile
0 250 500 750 Metres

Large Scale Pages 2-3
1:3,960 16 inches (40.64cm) to 1 mile 25.4cm to 1km
0 ¼ ½ Mile
0 250 500 750 Metres

Geographers' A-Z Map Company Limited

Head Office :
Fairfield Road, Borough Green, Sevenoaks, Kent TN15 8PP
Tel: 01732 781000
Showrooms :
44 Gray's Inn Road, London WC1X 8HX
Tel: 020 7440 9500

EDITION 1 2000

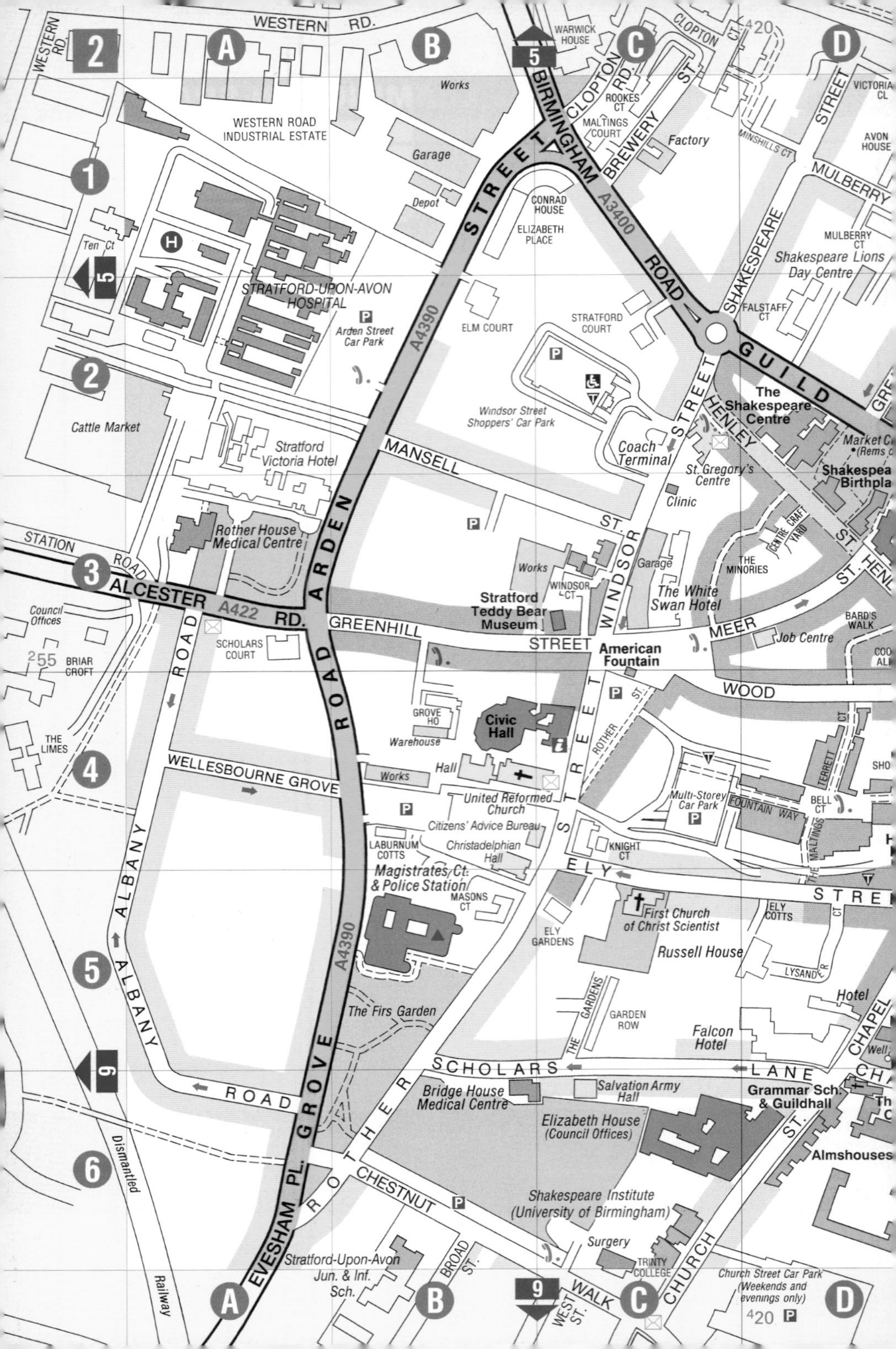

2
WESTERN RD.
WESTERN RD.
A
B
C
D
5
Works
WESTERN ROAD INDUSTRIAL ESTATE
Garage
Depot
WARWICK HOUSE
CLOPTON CT.
420
CLOPTON RD.
ROOKES CT
MALTINGS COURT
BREWERY ST.
Factory
MINSHILLS CT
STREET
VICTORIA CL
AVON HOUSE
MULBERRY
MULBERRY CT
Shakespeare Lions Day Centre
SHAKESPEARE
FALSTAFF CT
BIRMINGHAM
A3400
ROAD
STREET
CONRAD HOUSE
ELIZABETH PLACE
1
Ten Ct
5
STRATFORD-UPON-AVON HOSPITAL
Arden Street Car Park
A4390
ELM COURT
STRATFORD COURT
GUILD
2
Cattle Market
Stratford Victoria Hotel
Windsor Street Shoppers' Car Park
Coach Terminal
The Shakespeare Centre
HENLEY
STREET
Market C (Rems o
Shakespea Birthpla
MANSELL
ST.
St. Gregory's Centre
Clinic
ARDEN
STATION ROAD
Rother House Medical Centre
Works
WINDSOR CT
WINDSOR
Garage
CENTRE CRAFT YARD
THE MINORIES
ST. HENL
3
ALCESTER
A422
RD.
Stratford Teddy Bear Museum
The White Swan Hotel
Council Offices
255
BRIAR CROFT
ROAD
SCHOLARS COURT
GREENHILL
STREET
MEER
American Fountain
Job Centre
BARD'S WALK
COO AL
WOOD
ST.
ROTHER
ROAD
GROVE HO
Civic Hall
Warehouse
THE LIMES
4
WELLESBOURNE GROVE
Works
Hall
United Reformed Church
STREET
Multi-Storey Car Park
TERRETT CT
FOUNTAIN WAY
BELL CT
SHO
Citizens' Advice Bureau
LABURNUM COTTS
Christadelphian Hall
KNIGHT CT
THE MALTINGS
ALBANY
Magistrates Ct. & Police Station
MASONS CT
ELY
STREET
ELY COTTS
First Church of Christ Scientist
A4390
ELY GARDENS
Russell House
LYSANDER CT
5
ALBANY
The Firs Garden
THE GARDENS
GARDEN ROW
Hotel
Falcon Hotel
CHAPEL
Well
9
SCHOLARS
LANE
ROAD
GROVE
ROTHER
Bridge House Medical Centre
Salvation Army Hall
Grammar Sch. & Guildhall
Elizabeth House (Council Offices)
ST.
Almshouses
6
Dismantled
EVESHAM PL.
CHESTNUT
WALK
Shakespeare Institute (University of Birmingham)
Surgery
TRINITY COLLEGE
CHURCH
Stratford-Upon-Avon Jun. & Inf. Sch.
BROAD ST.
WEST ST.
Church Street Car Park (Weekends and evenings only)
420
Railway
A
B
9
C
D

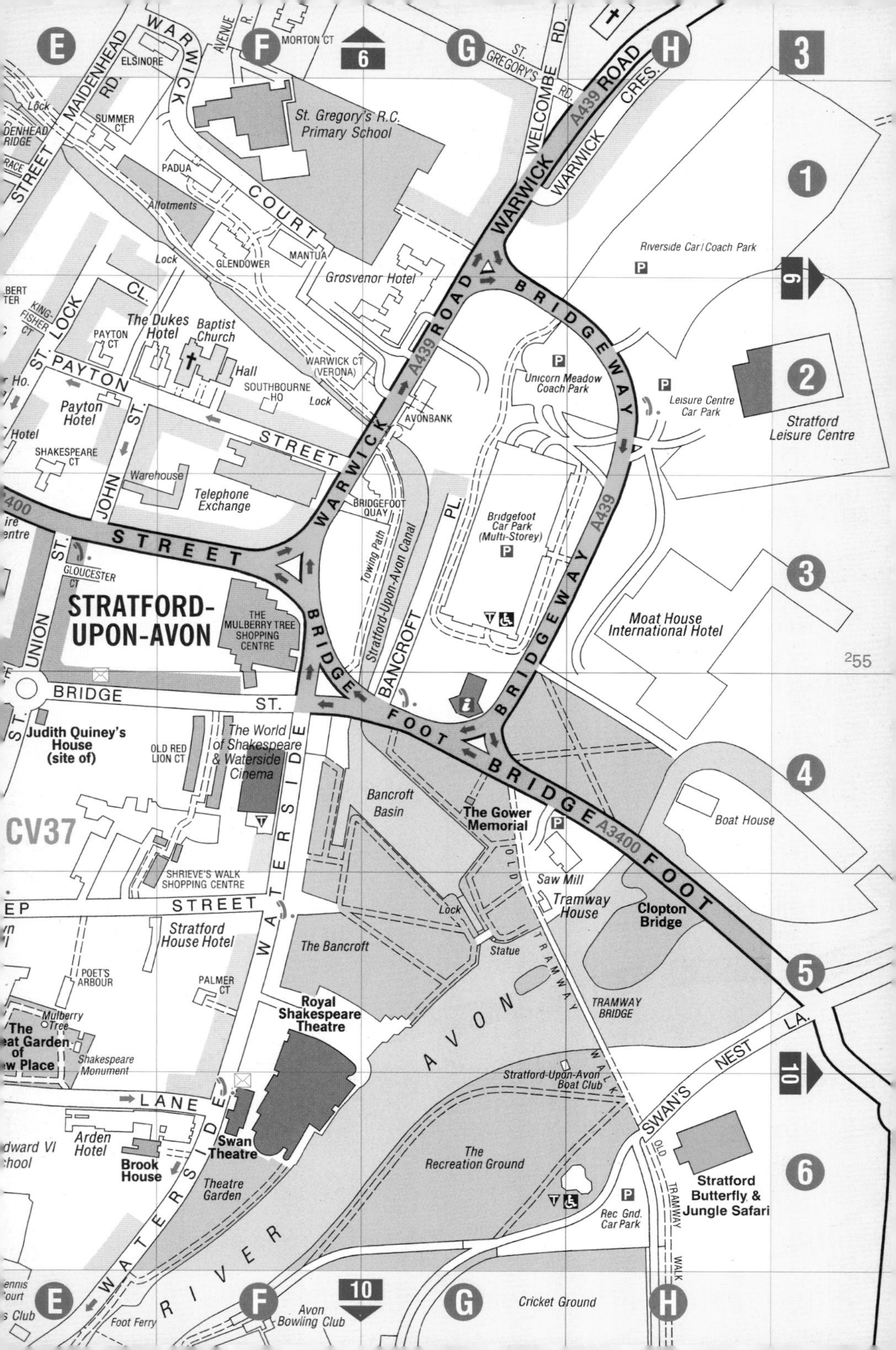

STRATFORD-UPON-AVON
CV37
St. Gregory's R.C. Primary School
Grosvenor Hotel
The Dukes Hotel
Baptist Church
Hall
Payton Hotel
Telephone Exchange
Warehouse
THE MULBERRY TREE SHOPPING CENTRE
Judith Quiney's House (site of)
The World of Shakespeare & Waterside Cinema
SHRIEVE'S WALK SHOPPING CENTRE
Stratford House Hotel
Royal Shakespeare Theatre
Swan Theatre
Brook House
Arden Hotel
Shakespeare Monument
Theatre Garden
Bancroft Basin
The Bancroft
The Gower Memorial
Statue
Saw Mill
Tramway House
Clopton Bridge
TRAMWAY BRIDGE
Stratford-Upon-Avon Boat Club
The Recreation Ground
Rec Gnd. Car Park
Stratford Butterfly & Jungle Safari
Cricket Ground
Avon Bowling Club
Foot Ferry
Riverside Car/Coach Park
Unicorn Meadow Coach Park
Leisure Centre Car Park
Stratford Leisure Centre
Bridgefoot Car Park (Multi-Storey)
Moat House International Hotel
Boat House
WARWICK ROAD
BRIDGEWAY
BRIDGE FOOT
BRIDGE STREET
BRIDGE ST.
WATERSIDE
RIVER AVON
SWAN'S NEST LA.
WARWICK COURT
Stratford-Upon-Avon Canal
Towing Path
BANCROFT PL.
A439
A3400
255

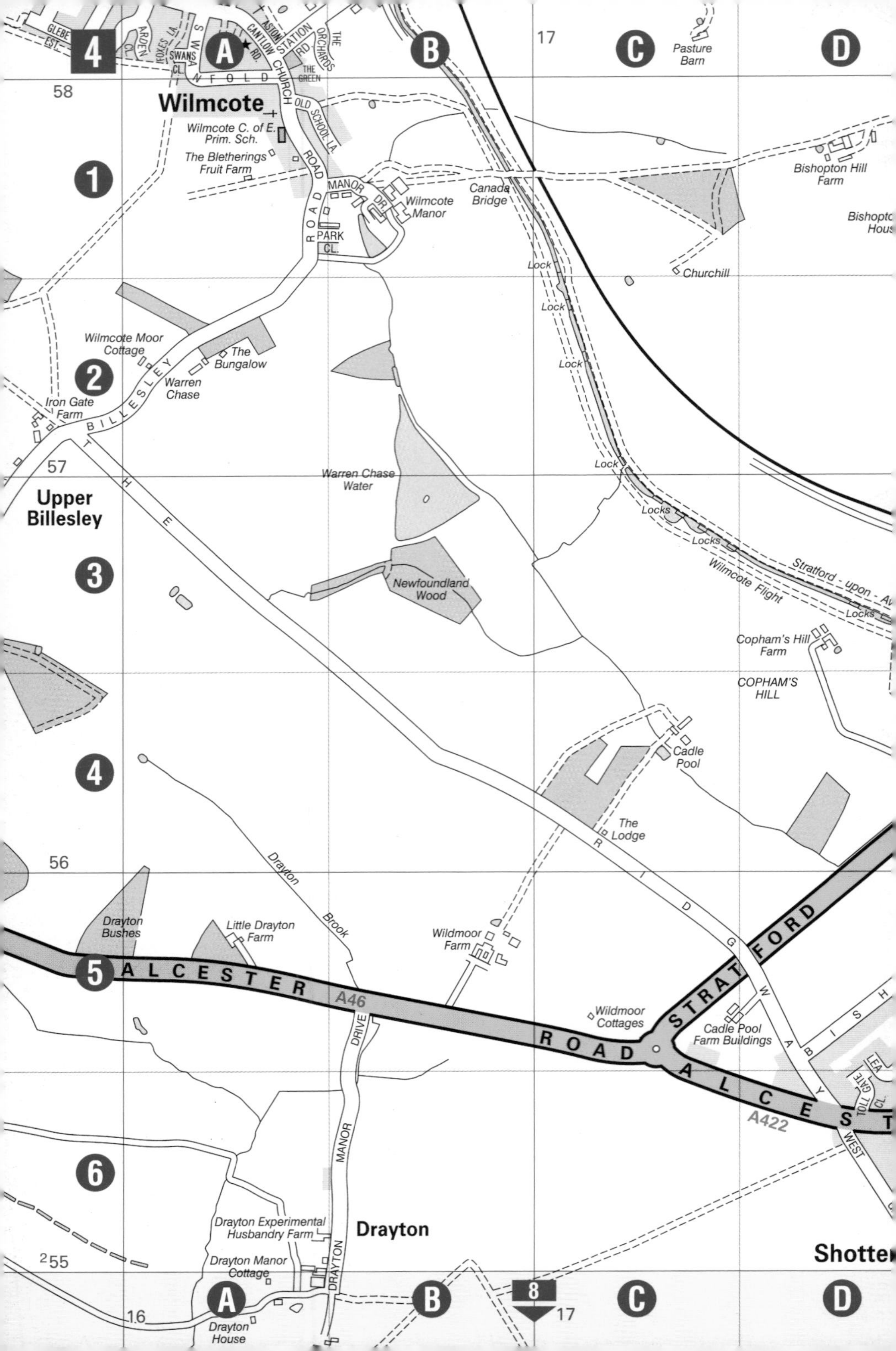

4
Wilmcote
Wilmcote C. of E. Prim. Sch.
The Bletherings Fruit Farm
Wilmcote Manor
Canada Bridge
Pasture Barn
Bishopton Hill Farm
Churchill
Lock
Locks
Wilmcote Flight
Stratford - upon - Av
Wilmcote Moor Cottage
The Bungalow
Warren Chase
Iron Gate Farm
BILLESLEY
Upper Billesley
Warren Chase Water
Newfoundland Wood
Copham's Hill Farm
COPHAM'S HILL
Cadle Pool
The Lodge
THE RIDGWAY
Drayton Brook
Drayton Bushes
Little Drayton Farm
Wildmoor Farm
Wildmoor Cottages
Cadle Pool Farm Buildings
ALCESTER A46 ROAD
STRATFORD
ALCESTER A422
DRIVE
MANOR
DRAYTON
Drayton
Drayton Experimental Husbandry Farm
Drayton Manor Cottage
Drayton House
Shotter
GLEBE EST.
ARDEN CL.
FOXES LA.
SWANS CL.
SWANFOLD
ASTON CANTLOW RD.
STATION RD.
THE ORCHARDS
THE GREEN
CHURCH ROAD
OLD SCHOOL LA.
MANOR DR.
PARK CL.
TOLL GATE CL.
LEA
WEST
BISH
58
57
56
55
16
17
8
A
B
C
D
1
2
3
4
5
6

STRATFORD-UPON-AVON
Lower Clopton
Bishopton
CV37
BIRMINGHAM (BISHOPTON HILL) ROAD
A3400
KINGS BY-PASS
A46
KINGS LANE
BIRMINGHAM ROAD
Park Wood
Park Farm
Little Acres
Round House Farm
Emms Cottages
Langley Farm
Hollincroft
Kings Acre
Clopton Cottages
Lower Clopton Farm
White House
Manor Farm
Burton Cottages
Stony Hill Covert
Gable Cottage
Clopton House
Egg Packing Station
Bishopton Lodge
Lower Lodge
The Pump House
Linden House
Avenue House
Spa Farm
Superstore
MAYBIRD CENTRE
PARK & RIDE
Works
Lambert School
Thomas Jolyffe Primary School
Shottery Brook
Lock
Playground
Bishopton Jun. & Inf. Sch.
Childrens Cen.
Comm. Cen.
Playing Field
Marie Corelli Special Sch.
Ball Courts
STRATFORD-UPON-AVON CANAL
Towing Path
Football Ground
STRATFORD-UPON-AVON HOSPITAL
Tennis Cts.
Cattle Mkt.
Med. Cen.
Coun. Off.
Mus.
Civic Hall
Council Offs.
Stratford-upon-Avon College
Stratford High Sch.
The Willows C.of E. Prim. Sch.
Playing Field
The Lodge
Shottery Hall
HATHAWAY HAMLET
A422
ALCESTER ROAD
MASONS ROAD
AVENUE FARM IND. EST.
TIMOTHY'S BRIDGE RD. IND. EST.
MASONS RD. INDUSTRIAL ESTATE
MAYBROOK IND. EST.
WESTERN RD. IND. EST.

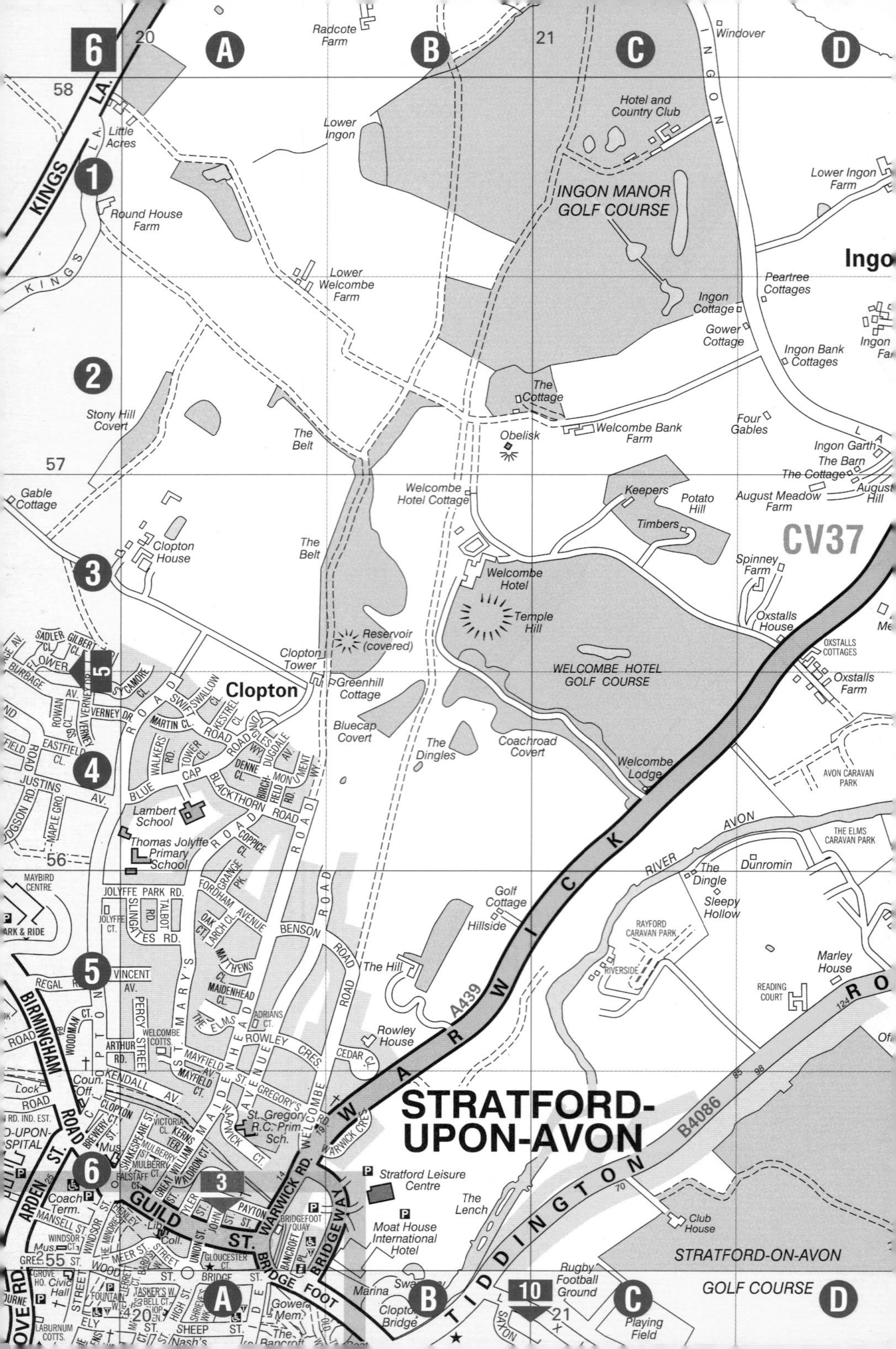

Radcote Farm
Windover
Hotel and Country Club
Lower Ingon
Little Acres
KINGS LA.
Round House Farm
INGON MANOR GOLF COURSE
Lower Ingon Farm
Ingon
Lower Welcombe Farm
Peartree Cottages
Ingon Cottage
Gower Cottage
Ingon Bank Cottages
Stony Hill Covert
The Cottage
The Belt
Obelisk
Welcombe Bank Farm
Four Gables
Ingon Garth
The Barn
The Cottage
Gable Cottage
Welcombe Hotel Cottage
Keepers
Potato Hill
August Meadow Farm
August Hill
Timbers
Clopton House
CV37
Spinney Farm
Welcombe Hotel
Temple Hill
Oxstalls House
Reservoir (covered)
OXSTALLS COTTAGES
Oxstalls Farm
Clopton Tower
WELCOMBE HOTEL GOLF COURSE
Clopton
Greenhill Cottage
Bluecap Covert
The Dingles
Coachroad Covert
Welcombe Lodge
AVON CARAVAN PARK
Lambert School
Thomas Jolyffe Primary School
RIVER AVON
THE ELMS CARAVAN PARK
MAYBIRD CENTRE
The Dingle
Dunromin
Golf Cottage
Sleepy Hollow
Hillside
RAYFORD CARAVAN PARK
RIVERSIDE
The Hill
Marley House
READING COURT
A439
WARWICK RD.
Rowley House
STRATFORD-UPON-AVON
B4086
TIDDINGTON RD.
St. Gregory's R.C. Prim. Sch.
Stratford Leisure Centre
The Lench
Coach Term.
Moat House International Hotel
Club House
STRATFORD-ON-AVON GOLF COURSE
Rugby Football Ground
Marina
Clopton Bridge
Playing Field
GUILD ST.
BRIDGE FOOT
BRIDGEWAY
BIRMINGHAM ROAD
CLOPTON ROAD
ARDEN ST.
Civic Hall

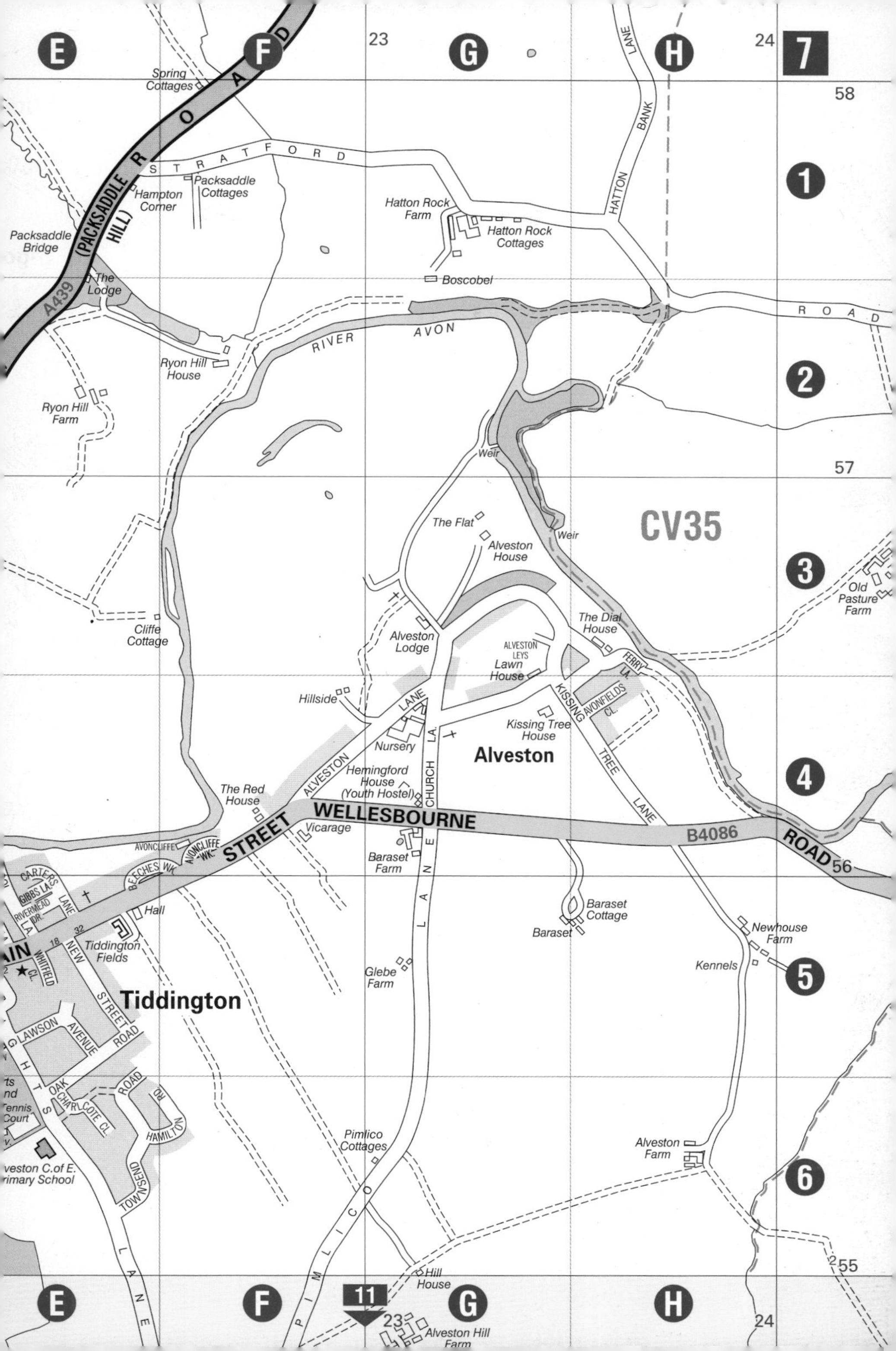

E
F
G
H
23
24
58
57
56
55
1
2
3
4
5
6
CV35
Alveston
Tiddington
STRATFORD ROAD
PACKSADDLE HILL
A439
Spring Cottages
Packsaddle Cottages
Hampton Corner
Packsaddle Bridge
The Lodge
Ryon Hill House
Ryon Hill Farm
Cliffe Cottage
RIVER AVON
HATTON BANK LANE
Hatton Rock Farm
Hatton Rock Cottages
Boscobel
ROAD
Weir
The Flat
Alveston House
Old Pasture Farm
Alveston Lodge
ALVESTON LEYS
Lawn House
The Dial House
FERRY LA.
AVONFIELDS CL.
Hillside
Nursery
KISSING TREE LANE
Kissing Tree House
ALVESTON LANE
CHURCH LA.
Hemingford House (Youth Hostel)
The Red House
WELLESBOURNE
STREET
B4086
ROAD
Vicarage
AVONCLIFFE
AVONCLIFFE WK.
BEECHES WK.
Baraset Farm
CARTERS LANE
GIBBS LA.
RIVERMEAD DR.
Hall
Tiddington Fields
NEW STREET
WHITFIELD CL.
LAWSON AVENUE
ROAD
OAK
CHARLCOTE CL.
ROAD
HAMILTON RD.
TOWNSEND
Alveston C.of E. Primary School
Baraset Cottage
Baraset
Newhouse Farm
Kennels
Glebe Farm
Pimlico Cottages
PIMLICO LANE
Alveston Farm
Hill House
11
Alveston Hill Farm

16
A
Drayton Experimental
Husbandry Farm
Drayton Manor
Cottage
DRAYTON MANOR DR.
B
Drayton
4
17
C
D
Shot
255
Drayton
House
Drayton
Farm
1
Hansells
Farm
Gretel
House
The
Triangle
BORDON
HILL
Brook
2
Drayton
Bordon
Wood
Reservoir
Sun
Dial
Greenhills
Dodwell
Dodwell
Cottages
54
R O A
The
Paddock
Heathcroft
EVESHAM B439
THE CIRCUIT
DODWELL
TRAILER PARK
Bordon
Nurseri
3
Little Hill
Farm
CV37
Ouse Brook
4
Little
Luddington
Sandfields
Farm
LUDD
Riverside
53
Sandfields
Cottages
Fairways
Avon Hill
5
Broadacre
Boddington
Farm
Hall
Manor
Farm
CHURCH CL.
MANOR FARM COTTS.
Avon Dell
Luddington
The Greenway Nature Trail
Experimental
Horticulture Station
Avondale
Milcote
Manor
Milcote
Cottages
Farm
House
Burnthous
Barn
6
Field Barn
Cottage
52
Glebe
Farm
Avonbourne
Greville
Mount
A
B
C
D
16
17

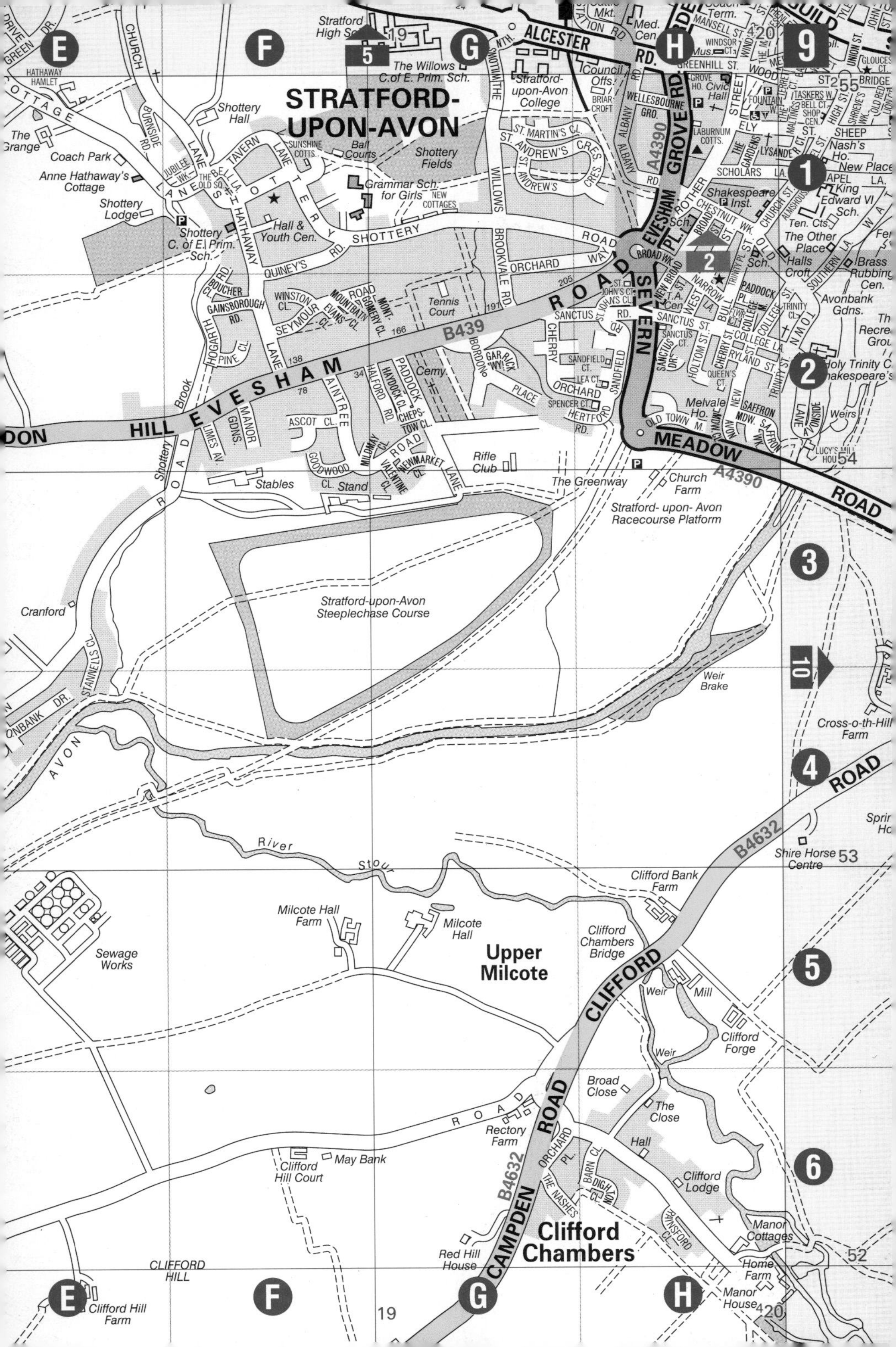
STRATFORD-
UPON-AVON
Shottery Fields
Grammar Sch. for Girls
Anne Hathaway's Cottage
Shottery Lodge
Shottery Hall
Coach Park
The Grange
Hathaway Hamlet
Shottery C. of E. Prim. Sch.
Hall & Youth Cen.
Stratford-upon-Avon College
The Willows C.of E. Prim. Sch.
Stratford High Sch.
Council Offs.
Shakespeare Inst.
King Edward VI Sch.
The Other Place
Halls Croft
Brass Rubbing Cen.
Avonbank Gdns.
Holy Trinity Ch.
Tennis Court
Cemy.
Rifle Club
Stables
Stand
The Greenway
Church Farm
Stratford- upon- Avon Racecourse Platform
Stratford-upon-Avon Steeplechase Course
Cranford
Weir Brake
Cross-o-th-Hill Farm
Shire Horse Centre
River Stour
Clifford Bank Farm
Milcote Hall Farm
Milcote Hall
Upper Milcote
Clifford Chambers Bridge
Sewage Works
Mill
Weir
Clifford Forge
Broad Close
The Close
Hall
Rectory Farm
Clifford Hill Court
May Bank
Clifford Lodge
Clifford Chambers
Red Hill House
Manor Cottages
Home Farm
Manor House
CLIFFORD HILL
Clifford Hill Farm
EVESHAM ROAD
B439
HILL
ALCESTER RD.
MEADOW ROAD
A4390
CLIFFORD ROAD
CAMPDEN ROAD
B4632
SHOTTERY RD.
A4390
EVESHAM PL.
GROVE RD.
SEVERN
RIVER AVON
E
F
G
H
1
2
3
4
5
6
5
9
10
2
19
420
55
54
53
52

10
A
B
C
D
1
2
3
4
5
6
STRATFORD-UPON-AVON
Bridge Town
CV37
STRATFORD-ON-AVON GOLF COURSE
Rugby Football Ground
Playing Field
Playing Fields
Pavilion
Club House
The Lench
Moat House International Hotel
Marina
Swannery
Clopton Bridge
TIDDINGTON RD.
B4086
BRIDGE FOOT
BRIDGEWAY
BRIDGEFOOT QUAY
BANCROFT PL.
LOXLEY ROAD
SAXON CL.
BEECH CL.
MANOR ROAD
BANBURY ROAD
A422
Gower Mem.
The Bancroft
Boat Club
Boat Ho.
Royal Shakespeare Theatre
Butterfly & Jungle Safari
Cricket Ground
Pavilion
Sports Ground
Bowls
Putting Grn.
Brass Rubbing Cen.
Avonbank Gdns.
The Recreation Ground
Holy Trinity Church (Shakespeare's Tomb)
Weir
Weirs
LUCY'S MILL HOUSES
SWAN'S NEST LA.
OLD TRAMWAY WALK
TRAMWAY
Nash's Ho.
New Place
King Edward VI Sch.
The Other Place
Ten. Cts.
Halls Croft
GUILD ST.
UNION ST.
JOHN ST.
WARWICK
STREET
BRIDGE ST.
SHEEP ST.
CHAPEL ST.
CHAPEL LA.
WATERSIDE
SOUTHERN LA.
CHURCH ST.
CHESTNUT WK.
SCHOLARS LA.
Shakespeare Inst.
ELY ST.
GROVE RD.
GREENHILL
MANSELL
Coach Term.
WINDSOR
Mus.
FOUNTAIN
TASKERS W.
BELL CT.
SHOP CEN.
SHRIEVE'S WK.
OLD RED LION CT.
ROTHER
BROAD ST.
NARROW LA.
WEST ST.
BULL ST.
PADDOCK PL.
COLLEGE LA.
COLLEGE M.
CHERRY ST.
HOLTOM ST.
TRINITY ST.
TRINITY CL.
MILL LANE
AVONSIDE
TOWN
Melvale Ho.
SAFFRON MDW.
SAFFRON WK.
NEW
SEVERN MEADOW ROAD
A4390
Church Farm
upon-Avon
Platform
LABURNUM COTTS.
LYSANDER CT.
ALMSHOUSES
HUNTS ROAD
KEATS RD.
BYRON ROAD
SHELLEY
MASEFIELD RD.
BRIDGETOWN ROAD
TENNYSON RD.
KIPLING ROAD
RUSHBROOK ROAD
Bridgetown Prim. Sch.
A3400
EVENLODE CL.
WINCOTT CL.
ETON ROAD
MANOR GREEN
DALE AVENUE
AVON CRESCENT
BURFORD RD.
MORETON CL.
SAINTSBURY CL.
EXHALL CL.
WATERLOO DR.
MILESTONE RD.
WATERLOO RISE
Bridgetown Farm
The Bungalow
Nursery
White House
Rush Brook
SHIPSTON ROAD
Springfield Cottages
Orchard Hill Cottages
Cross-o-th-Hill Farm
Springfield House
Shire Horse Centre
CLIFFORD ROAD
B4632
Weir Brake
Corporation Farm Cottages
Low Farm Cottages
Orchard Hill Farm
Mill
Clifford Forge
Clifford Lodge
Manor Cottages
Home Farm
Manor House
6
9
3
20
21
55
54
53
52
420

E
F
G
H
7
23
24
11
255
KNIGHTS
LANE
PIMLICO
LANE
Hill House
Alveston Hill Farm
1
ROAD
LOXLEY
BOUNDARY
HUNSCOTE
LANE
Arden Heath Farm
Bath Cottage
Alveston Hill
2
ROAD
ALVESTON PASTURES COTTAGES
Alveston Hill Cottages
Alveston Hill Farm No.1
Alveston Pastures
54
Chipping Court
3
The Crofts
4
Crofts Farm Cottages
LANE
53
Meer Hill
Heath Cottages
Little Crofts
Heath Farm
Crofts Cottages
5
A422
ROAD
Alveston Pasture
6
Claydons Farm
Hine's House
52
E
F
G
H
24
Goldicote House
Home Farm

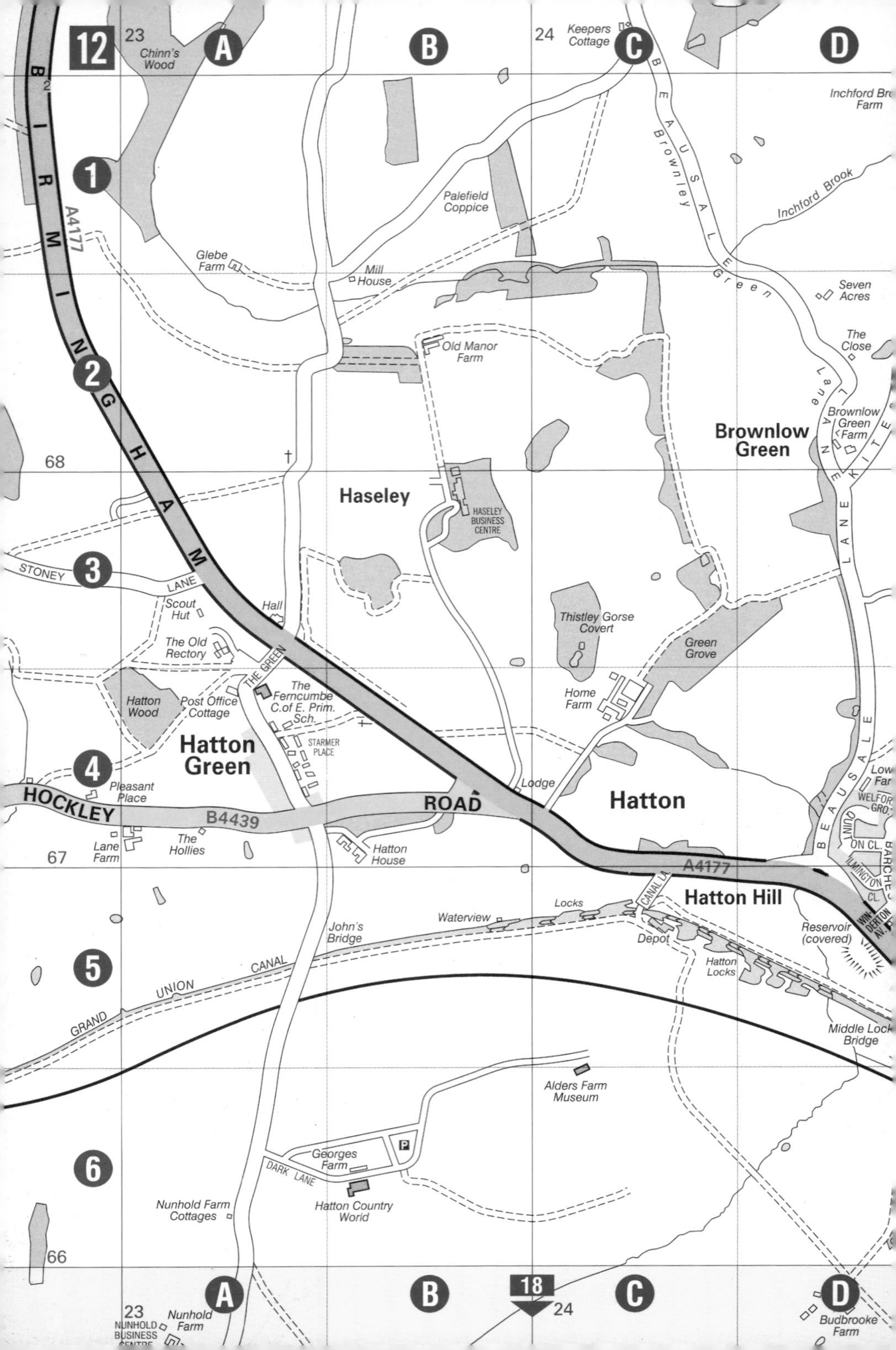
A
B
C
D
1
2
3
4
5
6
23
24
68
67
66
Chinn's Wood
Keepers Cottage
Inchford Brook Farm
Inchford Brook
Palefield Coppice
Glebe Farm
Mill House
Seven Acres
The Close
Old Manor Farm
Brownlow Green Farm
Brownlow Green
BIRMINGHAM
A4177
BEAUSALE
Brownley Green
Lane
KITE
LANE
Haseley
HASELEY BUSINESS CENTRE
STONEY LANE
Scout Hut
Hall
Thistley Gorse Covert
Green Grove
The Old Rectory
THE GREEN
The Ferncumbe C.of E. Prim. Sch.
Hatton Wood
Post Office Cottage
Home Farm
Hatton Green
STARMER PLACE
Pleasant Place
Lodge
Hatton
HOCKLEY
ROAD
B4439
Lane Farm
The Hollies
Hatton House
WELFORD GRO.
ON CL.
ILMINGTON CL.
Hatton Hill
CANAL LA.
Locks
Waterview
John's Bridge
Depot
Reservoir (covered)
WINDERTON AV.
Hatton Locks
GRAND UNION CANAL
Middle Lock Bridge
Alders Farm Museum
Georges Farm
P
DARK LANE
Hatton Country World
Nunhold Farm Cottages
18
Nunhold Farm
NUNHOLD BUSINESS CENTRE
Budbrooke Farm

13
E
F
26
G
H
27
WEDGNOCK
Bulloak Farm
Deer Park Farm
Old Park Cottages
LANE
WEDGNOCK
1
Larch Covert
DANGER AREA
2
Range Plantation
68
Kingstanding Farm
Deer Park Wood
DEER PARK
CV35
Keepers Cottages
Woodbine Cottages
3
Prospect Farm
Turkey Farm
WEDGNOCK OLD PARK
14
Blackbrake Plantation
4
DRIVE
DORSINGTON CL.
DRIVE
CHARINGWORTH
Smith's Covert
COMBROKE GRO.
EBRINGTON DR.
TIDMINGTON CL.
67
LANE
5
Wedgnock Park Farm
Locks
Lock House
Ugly Bridge
Brookside
Oaklands Farm
Lock
GRAND UNION CANAL
A4177 ROAD
6
A46
Warehouse
WEDGNOCK INDUSTRIAL ESTATE
RD.
66
Great Western Cottages
E
F
19
26
Lock
G
H
PRIVATE
27
Warwick Cemetery

CV8
CV34
Leek Wootton
Woodloes Park
The Cape
Goodrest Farm
Goodrest Lodge (site of)
Weir
Woodcote (County Police Headquarters)
Playing Field
Broome Close
Woodcote Dr.
Terrace Hill Wood
Nine Acre Plantation
Reservoir (covered)
Stone Edge Cottage
Stone Edge
Larch Covert
Gostee Spinney
Wootton Court Farm
Wootton Court
Danger Area
Range Plantation
Ash Plantation
Club House
Gaveston Wood Cottage
Prospect Farm
Wedgnock Rifle Range
Blacklow Hill
Middle Woodloes Cottages
Middle Woodloes
Lower Covert
Woodloes Farm
Loes Farm
Nursery
Wedgnock Lane
Warwick By-Pass
A46
Woodloes Lane
Primrose Hill
Hathaway Dr.
Woodloes Avenue North
Woodloes Avenue South
Wedgnock Industrial Estate
Broxell Close Industrial Est.
Warehouse
Rothwell Rd
Welton Rd
Wedgnock Park Bri.
Grand Union Canal Towing Path
Lock
Woodloes Jun. & Inf. Schs.
Comm. Cen.
Scar Bank
Millers Road
Guys Cross Pk. Rd
Warwick Hospital
Warwick Cemetery
Private Rd.
Cape Rd.
Lower Cape
Lock La.
Ladbroke Park
Broxell Cl.
Harris Rd.
Landor Rd.
Ridgeley Cl.
Eborall Cl.
Norton Dr.
Hughes Cl.
Baker Pl.
Crane Cl.
Corbison Cl.
Lowes Cl.
Lincoln Cl.
Gleeson Dr.
Suther Land Cl.
Kettlewell Cl.
Austwick Cl.
Buckden Cl.
Grassington Av.
Gisburn Cl.
Langcliffe Av.
Kirby Cl.
Cowper Cl.
Makepeace Av.
Hayle Av.
Edmondes Cl.
Neville Cl.
Pembroke Cl.
Arundel Cl.
Cornwall Cl.
Wade Gro.
Welsh Cl.
Wise Gro.
Eliot Cl.
Linden Cl.
Congreve Cl.
Yardley Cl.
Inchford Av.
Smythe Gro.
Greenway
Reardon Ct.
Warner Cl.
Twycross Wlk.
Raynsford Wlk.
Stanton Wlk.
Harmar Cl.
Handley Gro.
Boswell Gr.
Lacell Cl.
Sexham Cl.
Knoll Dr.
27
28
269
68
67
66
A
B
C
D
1
2
3
4
5
6
13
20

15
16
21
Hill Wootton
Old Milverton
Milverton
Guy's Cliffe
CV35
CV32
KENILWORTH BY-PASS
A46
B4115
WOOTTON ROAD
HILL WOOTTON ROAD
RIVER AVON
OLD MILVERTON LANE
OLD MILVERTON
RUGBY RD.
A445
WARWICK NEW ROAD
Wootton Spinnies
Woottonwood Farm
Sewage Works
Tower House
The Old Farm House
Hill Farm
Hill Wootton Farm
New House Farm
Marlpit Spinney
Meadow Cottage
Boat House
River Park
Clinic
Quarry Market Garden
Dropping Wells
Parkhouse Farm
Cottage Farm
Church Farm
Reading Room
Manor Farm
Guy's Cliffe House
Guy's Cliffe Stud
Dairy Farm
Playing Field
Weir
Mill Race
Trinity R.C. Sch.
Brookhurst Prim. Sch.
Sports Grd.
All Saints' C.E. Jun. Sch.
Portobello Bri.
Works
Cem.
THE FAIRWAYS
BEVERLEY ROAD
CLIFFE AVENUE
GUY'S CLIFFE ROAD
MILLBANK
GREVILLE
CRESCENT

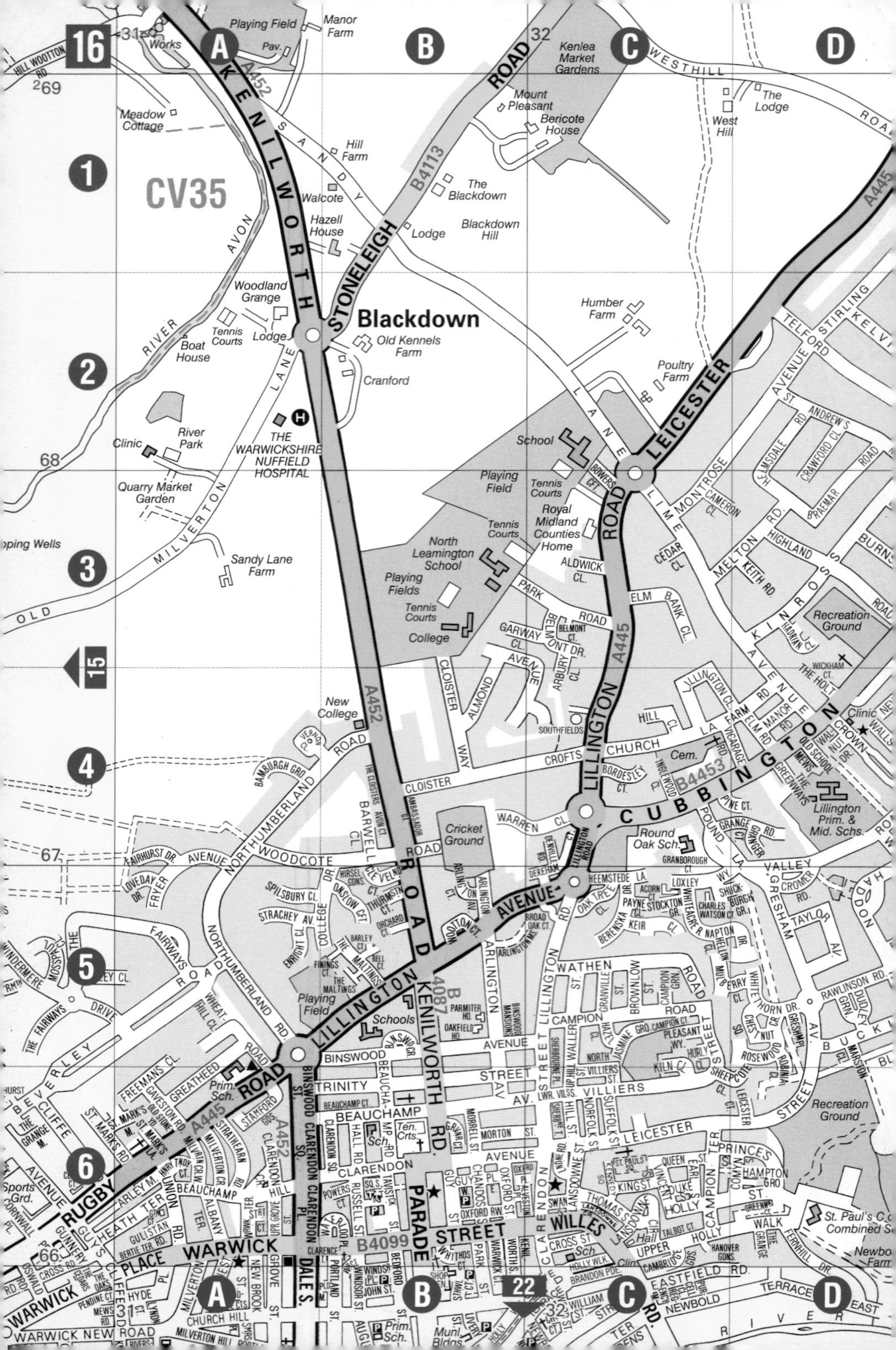

Blackdown
CV35
KENILWORTH ROAD
STONELEIGH ROAD
B4113
A452
SANDY LANE
WESTHILL ROAD
A445
LEICESTER ROAD
LILLINGTON ROAD
CUBBINGTON ROAD
B4453
LILLINGTON AVENUE
RUGBY ROAD
WARWICK PLACE
WARWICK STREET
PARADE
B4099
KENILWORTH RD.
B4087
WILLES ROAD
OLD MILVERTON ROAD
RIVER AVON
Playing Field
Manor Farm
Works
Kenlea Market Gardens
Mount Pleasant
Bericote House
The Lodge
West Hill
Meadow Cottage
Hill Farm
The Blackdown
Walcote
Hazell House
Lodge
Blackdown Hill
Woodland Grange
Tennis Courts
Boat House
Old Kennels Farm
Cranford
Humber Farm
Poultry Farm
River Park
Clinic
THE WARWICKSHIRE NUFFIELD HOSPITAL
Quarry Market Garden
Sandy Lane Farm
School
Playing Field
Royal Midland Counties Home
North Leamington School
Playing Fields
College
New College
Cricket Ground
Round Oak Sch.
Cem.
Lillington Prim. & Mid. Schs.
Recreation Ground
Schools
Prim. Sch.
Sports Grd.
St. Paul's C of E Combined Sch.
Newbold Farm
Munl. Bldgs.

15
22

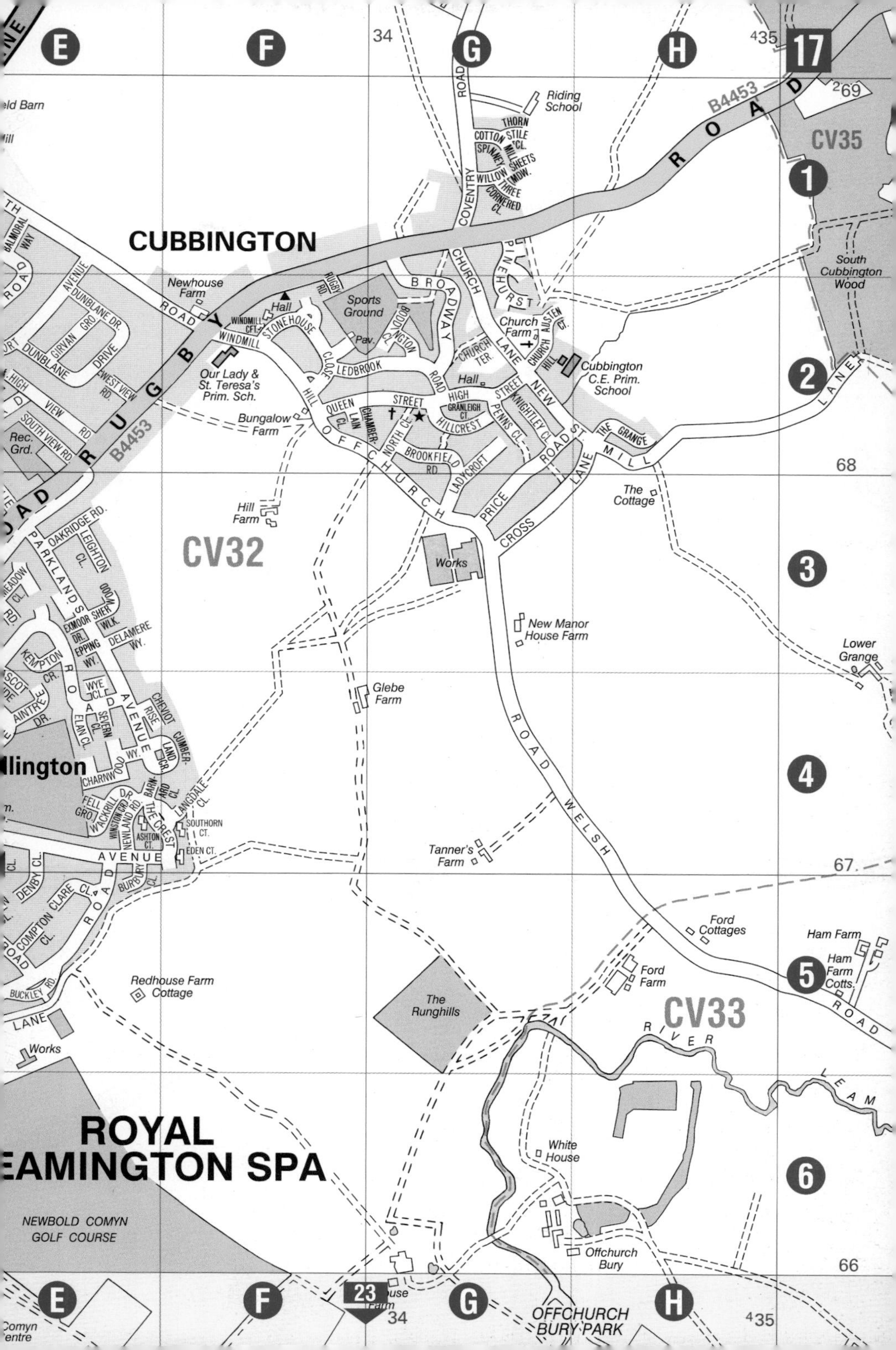
E
F
G
H
34
435
CV35
CV32
CV33
CUBBINGTON
ROYAL
LEAMINGTON SPA
NEWBOLD COMYN
GOLF COURSE
OFFCHURCH
BURY PARK
B4453
RUGBY ROAD
COVENTRY ROAD
BROADWAY
CHURCH LANE
NEW ST.
HIGH STREET
QUEEN STREET
OFFCHURCH LANE
WELSH ROAD
MILL LANE
CROSS ROAD
PRICE ROAD
LEDBROOK ROAD
BROOKFIELD RD
LADYCROFT
HILLCREST
PINEHURST
Riding School
Sports Ground
Pav.
Hall
Newhouse Farm
Our Lady & St. Teresa's Prim. Sch.
Bungalow Farm
Church Farm
Cubbington C.E. Prim. School
South Cubbington Wood
The Cottage
Hill Farm
Works
New Manor House Farm
Lower Grange
Glebe Farm
Tanner's Farm
Ford Cottages
Ford Farm
Ham Farm
Ham Farm Cotts.
Redhouse Farm Cottage
The Runghills
RIVER LEAM
White House
Offchurch Bury
Rec. Grd.
1
2
3
4
5
6
68
67
66
269
23

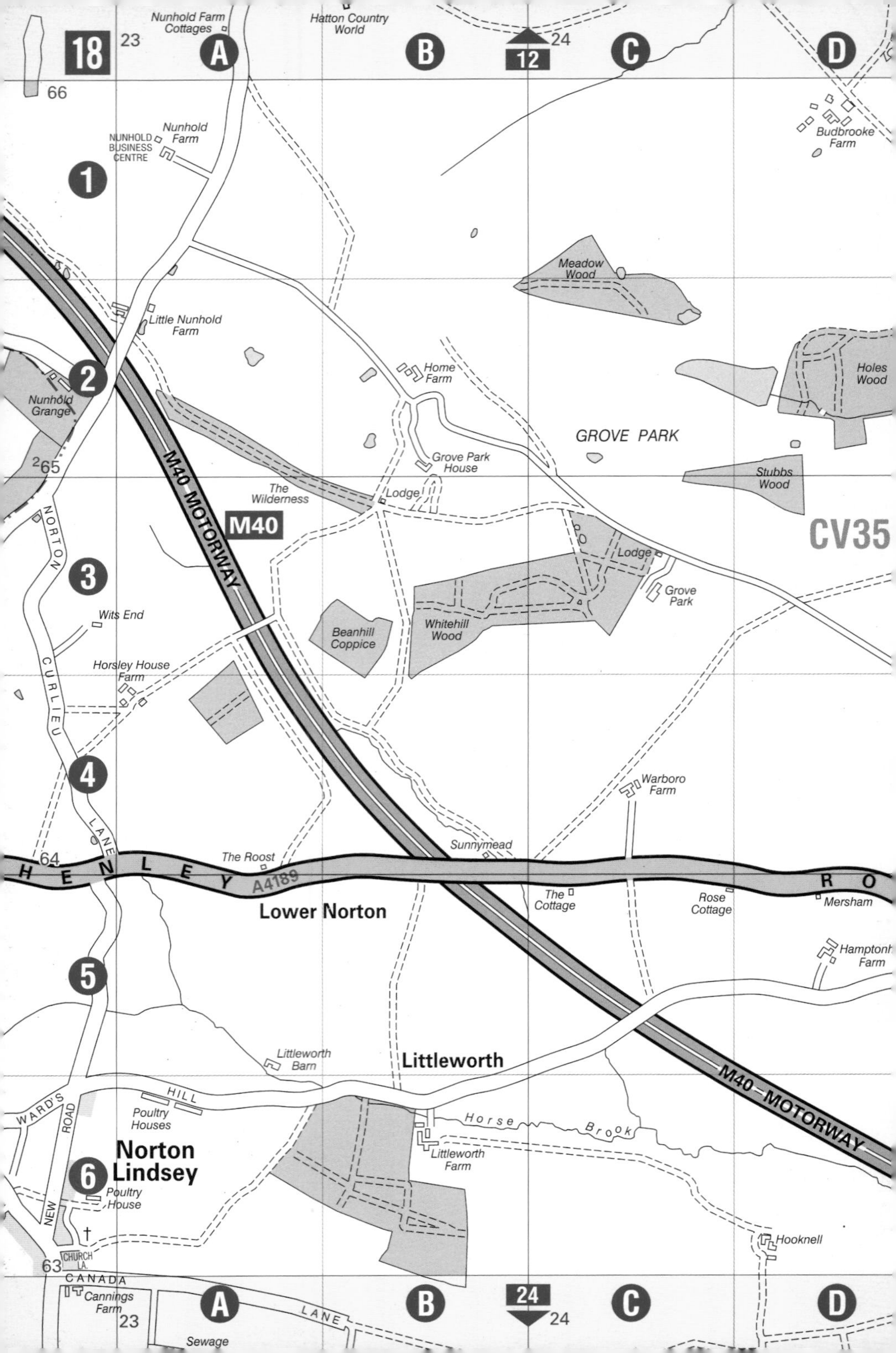
18
23
A
B
C
D
12
24
66
Nunhold Farm Cottages
Hatton Country World
NUNHOLD BUSINESS CENTRE
Nunhold Farm
Budbrooke Farm
1
2
3
4
5
6
Meadow Wood
Little Nunhold Farm
Nunhold Grange
Home Farm
Holes Wood
GROVE PARK
Grove Park House
Stubbs Wood
65
The Wilderness
Lodge
M40
M40 MOTORWAY
CV35
NORTON
Lodge
Grove Park
Wits End
Beanhill Coppice
Whitehill Wood
Horsley House Farm
CURLIEU
LANE
Warboro Farm
64
Sunnymead
The Roost
HENLEY ROAD
A4189
Lower Norton
The Cottage
Rose Cottage
Mersham
Hamptonh Farm
Littleworth Barn
Littleworth
WARD'S HILL
ROAD
Poultry Houses
Horse Brook
Norton Lindsey
Littleworth Farm
Poultry House
NEW
CHURCH LA.
Hooknell
63
CANADA LANE
Cannings Farm
Sewage

19
13
25
20
Budbrooke
Hampton Magna
Hampton on the Hill
CV34
WARWICK RACE COURSE
Great Western Cottages
Grange Farm
Church Farm
Oldence
Zaragoza
Stanks Farm
Sewage Works
Leasowes Farm
Warwick Cemetery
Birmingham Road Bri.
BUDBROOKE IND. EST.
AMHERST BUSINESS CENTRE
Comm. Cen.
Rec. Grd.
Budbrooke Prim. Sch.
Gog Bridge
Gog Brook Farm
Hampton Lodge
Horse Brook Bridge
Aylesford School
GRAND UNION CANAL
Lock
BIRMINGHAM ROAD
A4177
A46
A425
A4189
B4463
M40
HAMPTON ROAD
WARWICK BY-PASS
BUDBROOKE ROAD
WOODWAY
OLD WOODWAY
OLD SCHOOL LA.
Race Course
Gog Brook
Horse Brook
26
27
65
64
63
66

20
14
19
26
A
B
C
D
1
2
3
4
5
6
27
28
66
65
64
63
The Cape
WARWICK
Packmores
Bridge End
CV34
Warwick Cemetery
Birmingham Road Bri.
BIRMINGHAM ROAD
A425
SALTISFORD
Grand Union Canal
Wedgnock Park Bri.
Industrial Estate
BROXELL CLOSE INDUSTRIAL EST.
WEDGNOCK INDUS. EST.
BUDBROOKE IND. EST.
AMHERST BUSINESS CENTRE
ST. MICHAEL'S HOSP.
Saltisford Common
WARWICK HOSPITAL
Priory Ponds
St.Mary's R.C. Prim. Sch.
Warwick
Priory Park
The Priory
Clinics
Nursery Sch.
Race Course
WARWICK GOLF COURSE
Driving Range
Warwick Golf Cen.
Lammas Field
WARWICK RACE COURSE
Stands
Superstore
PRIORY
NORTHGATE
THE BUTTS
SMITH ST.
JURY ST.
HIGH ST.
CASTLE HILL
JOHNS
ST. NICHOLAS
COVENTRY
A429
BANBURY
WARWICK CASTLE
Weirs
Mill St.
BRIDGE END
St. John's Ho.
FRIARS ST.
HAMPTON ST.
HAMPTON ROAD
A4189
WEST ROAD
Sports Ground
Tennis Courts
Foxes Study
The Lilacs
Lord Brooke's Clump
Gog Bridge
Gog Brook
Newburgh Prim. Sch.
Aylesford School
Fisher's Bri.
Temple Hill Plantation
CASTLE PARK
Leafield Farm
Leafield Privet
Greenacre
Ashbeds Wood
Sewage Works
STRATFORD
Leafield Bridge
Lodge
Lodge Wood

21
15
27
430
E
F
G
H
1
2
3
4
5
6
CV32
CV31
Myton
Heathcote
Emscote Road A445
Rugby Rd.
Warwick New Rd.
B4099
Prince's Dr. A452
Park Dr.
Old Warwick Rd.
Myton Road A425
Europa Way A452
Banbury Road Hill A425
Gallows Hill
Heathcote Lane
Harbury Lane
Queensway
Tachbrook Park Drive
Charles Street Bridge
Emscote Inf. Sch.
Emscote Lawn Sch.
Emscote Bridge
Portobello Bri.
Potterton Works
Edmondscote Manor House
Sports Ground
Edmondscote Running Track
Recreation Ground
Warwickshire College
Council Offs.
Victoria Park
Tennis Crts.
Jephson's Farm
Riverside Walk
Leam Bri.
Mytton Hamlet
Hospice
Myton School
Trinity R.C. School
Brook Farm
Henry VIII Farm
Warwick School
Playing Field
The Shires Retail Park
Queensway Trading Estate
Hotel
Warwick Technology Park
Heathcote Hill Farm
Heathcote Industrial Estate
Factory
Hawkes Farm
Longacre
Lower Heathcote Farm
Temple Hill Spinney
Turnbulls Garden
Tach Brook
The Aspens
Asps Cottages

22
A
B
C
D
16
28
21
1
2
3
4
5
6
31
32
63
64
65
66
ROYAL
LEAMINGTON SPA
WHITNASH
Heathcote
CV34
Leamington Spa
WARWICK
WARWICK NEW ROAD
WARWICK PLACE
Warwickshire College
Council Offs.
Adelaide Bri.
Bowling Grns.
Tennis Crts.
VICTORIA PARK
ADELAIDE RD.
AVENUE RD.
PARK DR.
A452
PRINCES DR.
MYTON RD.
THE MOORINGS
EUROPA WAY
OLD WARWICK ROAD
A425
Grand Union Canal
Recreation Ground
St. John Sch.
Works
THE SHIRES RETAIL PARK
QUEENSWAY TRADING ESTATE
TACHBROOK PARK BUSINESS CENTRE
TACHBROOK PARK DRIVE
APOLLO WAY
ATHENA DRIVE
ARTEMIS DR.
HERMES CL.
Sports Ground
Pav.
Kingsway Prim. Sch.
St. Patrick's Prim. Sch.
TROJAN BUSINESS CEN.
TITAN BUSINESS CENTRE
SPARTAN CL.
DELPHI CL.
HEATHCOTE LANE
ROYAL LEAMINGTON SPA REHABILITATION HOSPITAL
OPHELIA DRIVE
OTHELLO AV.
IMOGEN GDNS.
BOLINGBROKE DR.
HARBURY LANE
Windmill (Dis.)
TACHBROOK ROAD
B4087
PARADE
Pump Room Gdns.
Mus. Lib.
Bus Sta.
STATION APP.
HIGH ST.
BATH ST.
Spa Centre
JEPHSON GDNS.
Mill Gdns.
Willes Bridge
Welch's Meadow
RIVER LEAM
WILLES RD.
B4099
NEWBOLD TERRACE
BRANDON PDE.
REGENT STREET
LEAM TERRACE
RUSSELL TER.
PLYMOUTH PL.
RADFORD ROAD
HOSP.
Clapham Ter. Prim. Sch.
Trading Estate
Recreation Ground
SYDENHAM INDUSTRIAL ESTATE
BRUNSWICK STREET
Clinic-Lib.
GROSVENOR RD.
PROSPECT RD.
ST. HELENS ROAD
WINDMILL RD.
Cemetery
SOUTHWAY
ST. MARGARET'S RD.
Whitnash Prim. Sch.
Comm. Cen.
Recreation Ground
Club
WHITNASH RD.
HEATHCOTE LANE
Lib.
FRANKLIN RD.
MOORHILL RD.
St. Joseph's Prim. Sch.
Briar Hill Inf. Sch.
St. Margaret's Middle Sch.
MORRIS DR.
Club House
ASHFORD RD.

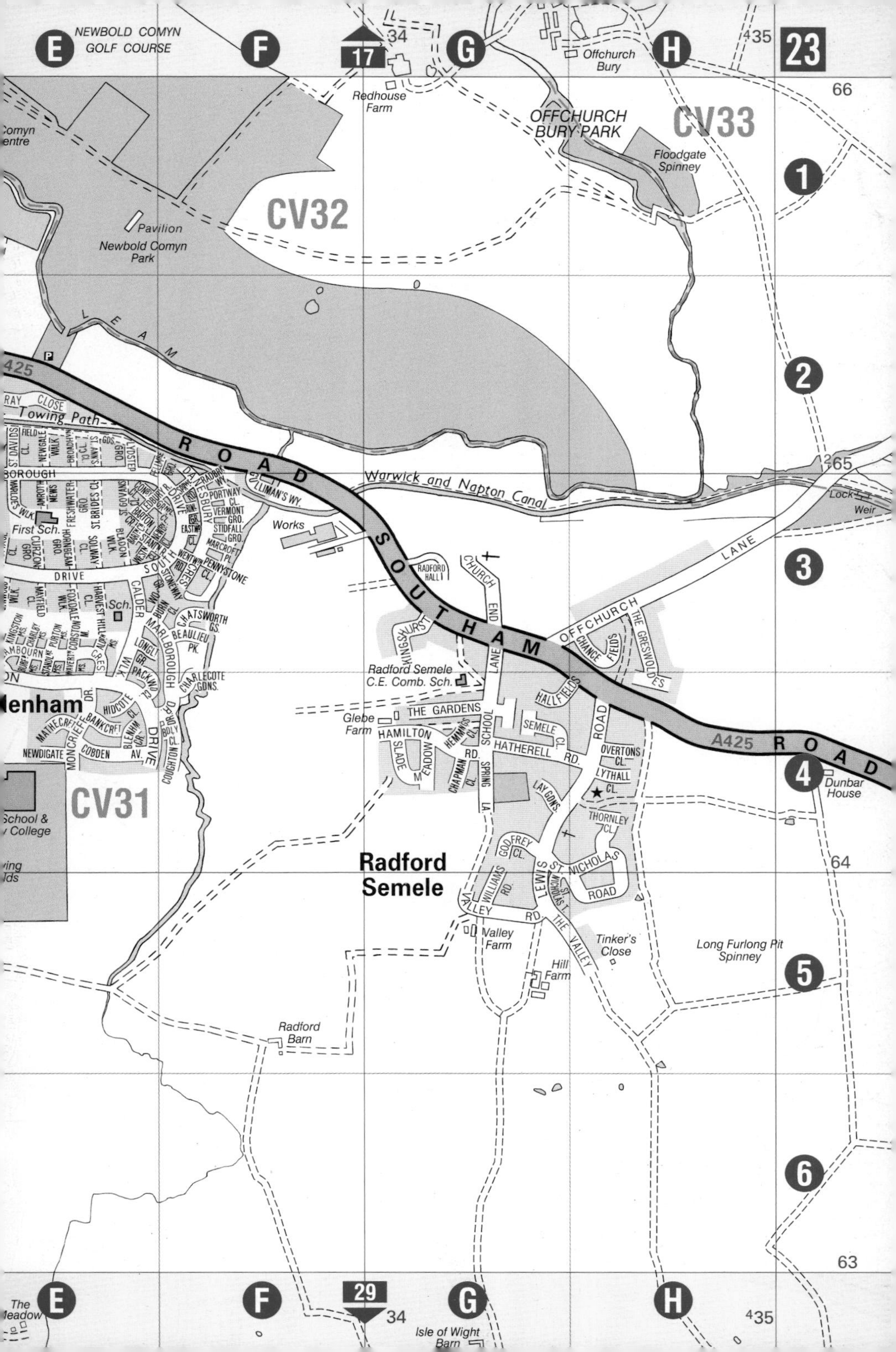

NEWBOLD COMYN GOLF COURSE
Redhouse Farm
Offchurch Bury
OFFCHURCH BURY PARK
CV33
Floodgate Spinney
CV32
Pavilion
Newbold Comyn Park
LEAM
A425
SOUTHAM ROAD
Towing Path
Warwick and Napton Canal
Lock
Weir
Works
First Sch.
Sch.
RADFORD HALL
CHURCH LANE
OFFCHURCH LANE
CHANCE FIELDS
THE GRESWOLDES
HALLFIELDS
KINGSHURST
Radford Semele C.E. Comb. Sch.
Glebe Farm
THE GARDENS
HAMILTON RD.
SLADE MEADOW
HEMMINGS CL.
SCHOOL LANE
SEMELE CL.
HATHERELL RD.
OVERTONS CL.
LYTHALL CL.
THORNLEY CL.
LAY GDNS.
CHAPMAN CL.
SPRING LA.
GODFREY CL.
WILLIAMS RD.
LEWIS RD.
ST. NICHOLAS ROAD
VALLEY RD.
THE VALLEY
Dunbar House
Radford Semele
Valley Farm
Hill Farm
Tinker's Close
Long Furlong Pit Spinney
Radford Barn
CV31
Isle of Wight Barn
The Meadow
MARLBOROUGH DRIVE
CHATSWORTH GS.
BEAULIEU PK.
CHARLECOTE GDNS.
HIDCOTE GR.
BANKCROFT
BLENHEIM CR.
MATHECROFT
MONCRIEFFE DR.
COBDEN AV.
NEWDIGATE
DANESBURY CRES.
PORTWAY CL.
VERMONT GRO.
STIDFALL GRO.
MARCROFT PL.
PENNYSTONE CL.
GULLIMAN'S WY.
SOUTH DRIVE
CALDER WLK.
HARVEST HILL CL.
SOLWAY GRO.
CURZON GRO.
FRESHWATER GRO.
ST. BRIDES CL.
HORNBEAM GRO.
MAYFIELD WLK.
FOXDALE WLK.
BOROUGH
RAY CLOSE
ST. DAVIDS CL.
NEWGALE WLK.
BROADHAVEN
LYDSTEP GRO.
KINGSTON MS.
CORSTON M.
PURTON MS.
School & College
E
F
G
H
1
2
3
4
5
6
17
29
34
435
66
65
64
63

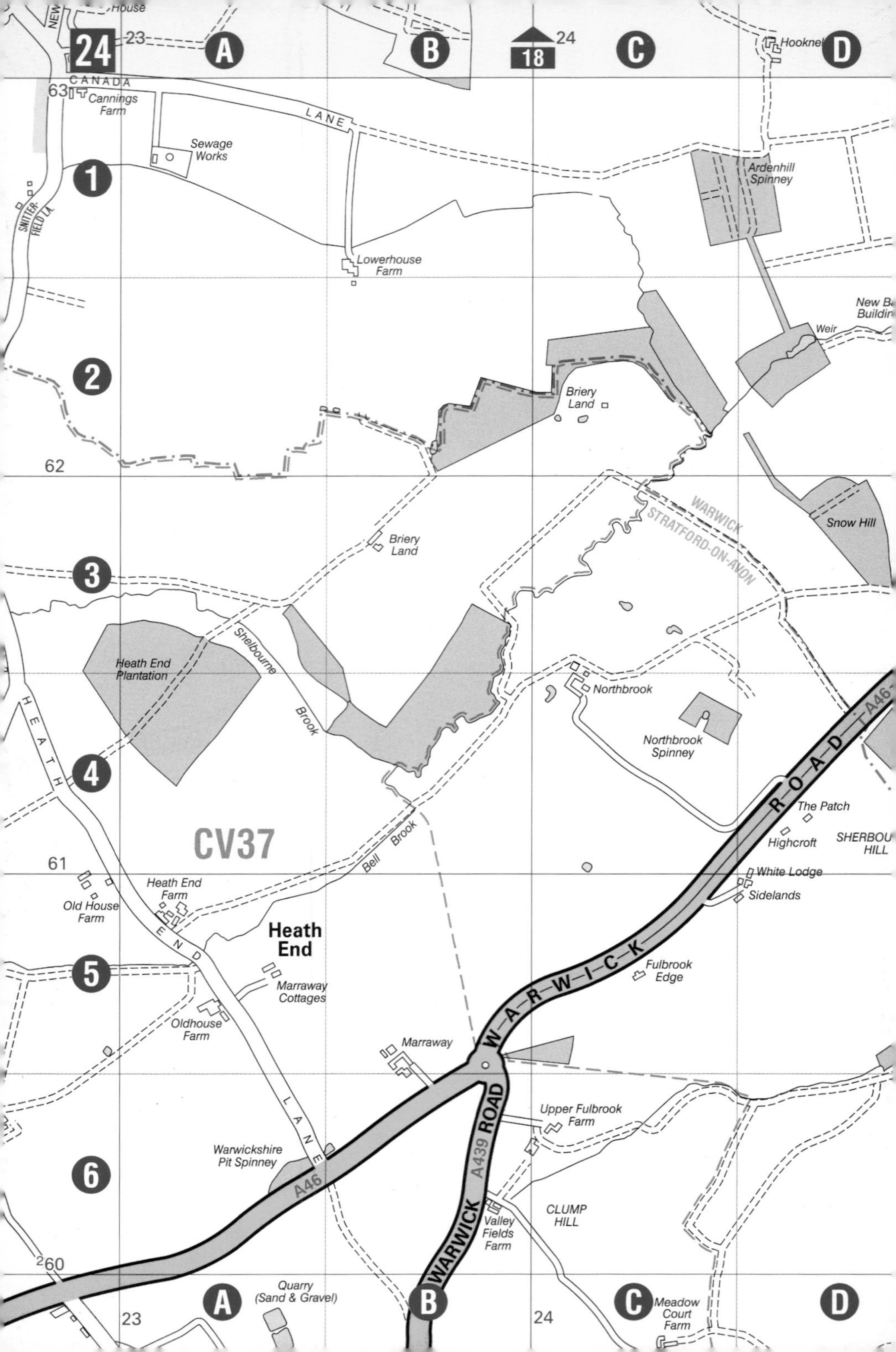
24
18
A
B
C
D
1
2
3
4
5
6
CANADA LANE
Cannings Farm
Sewage Works
SNITTERFIELD LA.
Lowerhouse Farm
Ardenhill Spinney
Hooknell
New B. Buildin
Weir
Briery Land
WARWICK
STRATFORD-ON-AVON
Snow Hill
Briery Land
Heath End Plantation
Shelbourne Brook
Northbrook
Northbrook Spinney
The Patch
Highcroft
SHERBOU HILL
White Lodge
Sidelands
CV37
Bell Brook
HEATH END LANE
Heath End Farm
Old House Farm
Heath End
Marraway Cottages
Oldhouse Farm
Fulbrook Edge
WARWICK ROAD
A46
Marraway
Upper Fulbrook Farm
Warwickshire Pit Spinney
A439
CLUMP HILL
Valley Fields Farm
Quarry (Sand & Gravel)
Meadow Court Farm
23
24
60
61
62
63

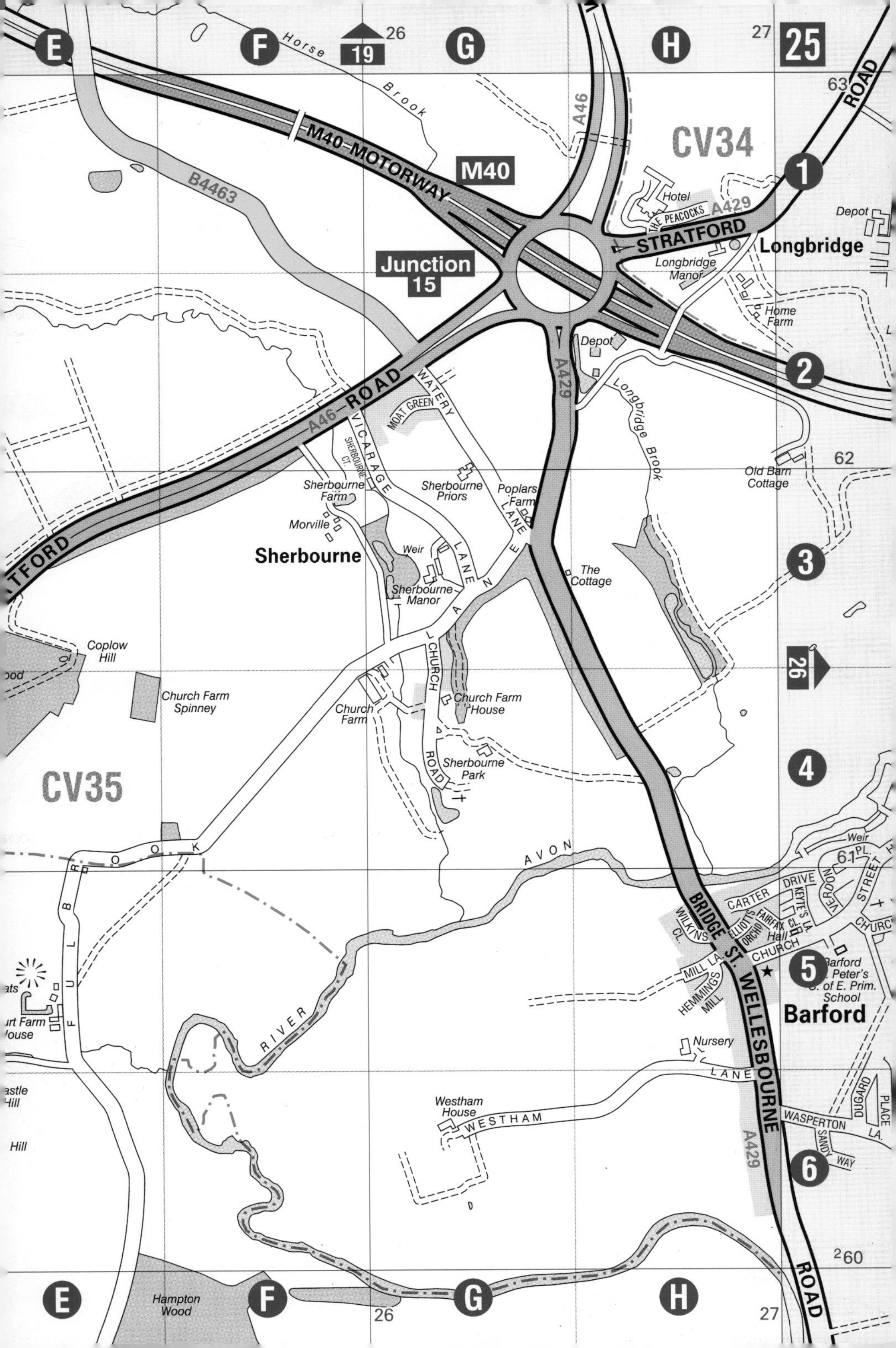
19
26
27
63
62
61
260
E
F
G
H
1
2
3
4
5
6
CV34
CV35
Horse Brook
M40 MOTORWAY
M40
Junction 15
B4463
A46
A429
STRATFORD ROAD
ROAD
Hotel
THE PEACOCKS
Depot
Longbridge
Longbridge Manor
Home Farm
A46 ROAD
WATERY LANE
MOAT GREEN
VICARAGE LANE
SHERBOURNE CT.
Longbridge Brook
Old Barn Cottage
Sherbourne Farm
Sherbourne Priors
Poplars Farm
Morville
Sherbourne
Weir
Sherbourne Manor
The Cottage
Coplow Hill
Church Farm Spinney
CHURCH ROAD
Church Farm
Church Farm House
Sherbourne Park
26
FULBROOK LANE
AVON
RIVER
BRIDGE ST.
WELLESBOURNE ROAD
CARTER DRIVE
KEYTE'S LA.
VERDON PL.
STREET
WILKINS CL.
ELLIOTTS ORCHD
FAIRFAX CL.
Hall
CHURCH
MILL LA.
HEMMINGS MILL
Barford St. Peter's C. of E. Prim. School
Barford
Nursery
LANE
Westham House
WESTHAM
WASPERTON LA.
SANDY WAY
DUGARD PLACE
Hampton Wood
Coplow Hill
Castle Hill
Hill
Court Farm House

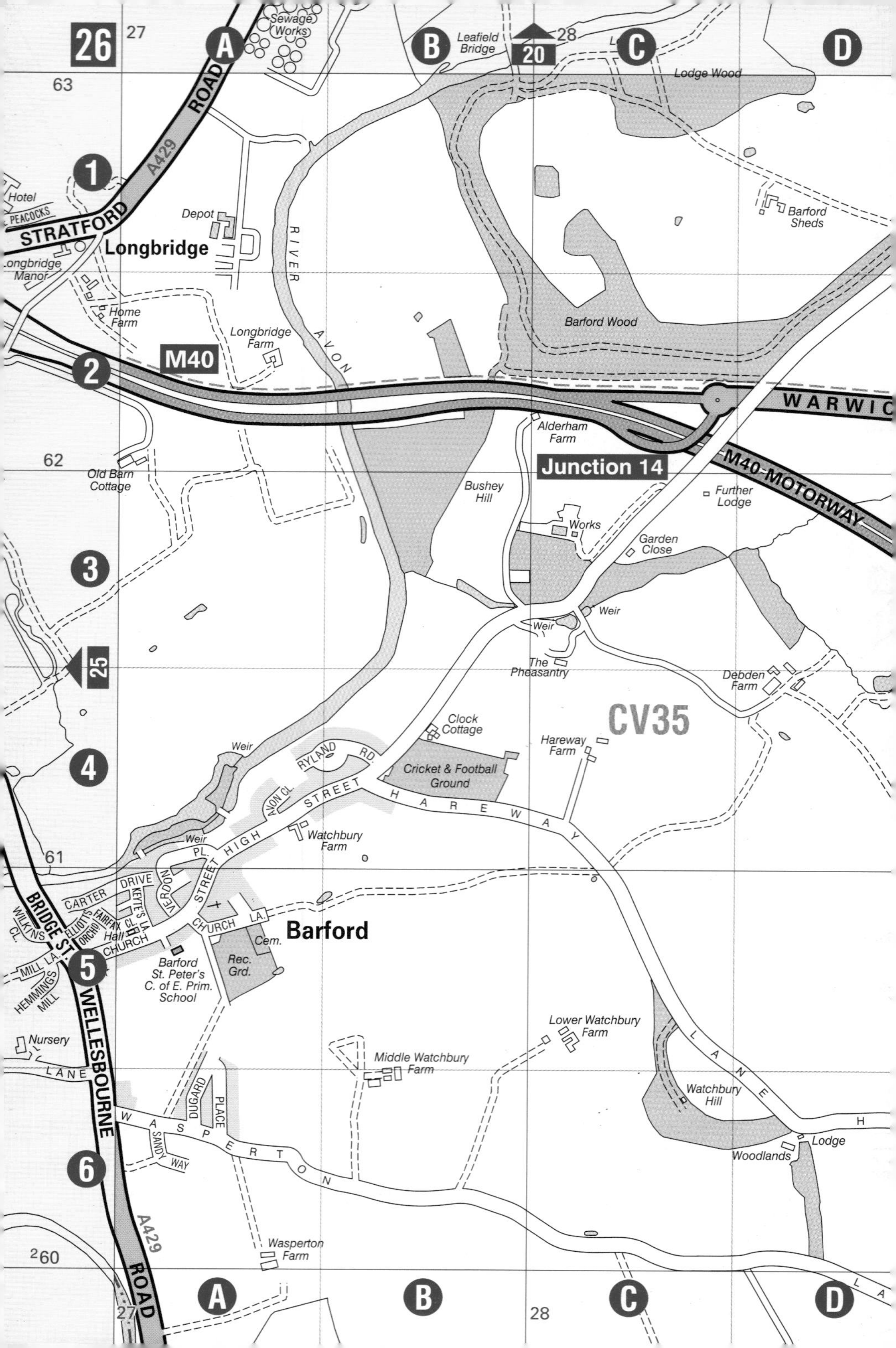

27
A
B
C
D
28
20
63
Sewage Works
Leafield Bridge
Lodge Wood
1
Hotel
PEACOCKS
STRATFORD
ROAD
A429
Depot
Longbridge
Longbridge Manor
Home Farm
Longbridge Farm
RIVER AVON
Barford Sheds
Barford Wood
M40
2
WARWIC
Alderham Farm
Junction 14
M40 MOTORWAY
62
Old Barn Cottage
Bushey Hill
Further Lodge
Works
Garden Close
3
Weir
Weir
Weir
The Pheasantry
25
Debden Farm
CV35
Clock Cottage
Hareway Farm
4
RYLAND RD.
Cricket & Football Ground
AVON CL.
HIGH STREET
HAREWAY
Watchbury Farm
61
VERDON PL.
CARTER DRIVE
KEYTE'S LA.
FAIRFAX CL.
ELLIOTTS ORCH.
WILKINS CL.
BRIDGE ST.
Hall
CHURCH LA.
Barford
Cem.
Rec. Grd.
5
MILL LA.
Barford St. Peter's C. of E. Prim. School
HEMMINGS MILL
WELLESBOURNE
Nursery
LANE
Lower Watchbury Farm
Middle Watchbury Farm
DUGARD PLACE
WASPERTON
SANDY WAY
Watchbury Hill
LANE
H
Lodge
Woodlands
6
A429
ROAD
Wasperton Farm
260
27
A
B
C
D
28
LA

E
F
21
430
G
H
27
Lower Heathcote Farm
The Aspens
Asps Cottages
BANBURY
A425
A452
EUROPA
WAY
CV34
Park Farm
ROAD
Depot
BY-PASS
Sewage Works
HARBURY LANE
TAMORA CL.
WILLOW CL.
BEECH CT.
CHESTNUT CT.
BIRCH CT.
1
2
62
New House Farm
3
Windmill Hill
M40
Spinney Farm
Half Moon Plantation
Greys Mallory
BANBURY
28
PENFOLD CL.
CROFT
ARGYLE WY.
FIELDS
DUNSTALL CR.
ST. CHADS
VICARAGE RISE
OVERBERRY ORCH.
PARSONAGE CL.
POWELL CL.
Nursery
Knob Hill
SEVEN ACRE CL.
Red House Farm
Red House Cottages
Brickyard Cottage
MALLORY
4
HOLT
BRADFORD CL.
KINGSLEY COURT CL.
HASSALL CL.
KINGSLEY RD.
ROAD
School
THE LEES
AVENUE
61
CV33
Bishop's Tachbrook
Gooseberry Hall Farm
Tachbrook Hill Farm
5
ROAD
LANE
A452
Plestowes Spinney
WAY
WOOD
Junction 13
M40-MOTORWAY
M40
6
Oakley Wood Farm
ROAD
B4100
Plestowes Farm
Plestowes House
B4087
OAKLEY
260
E
F
G
B4087
H
430
31

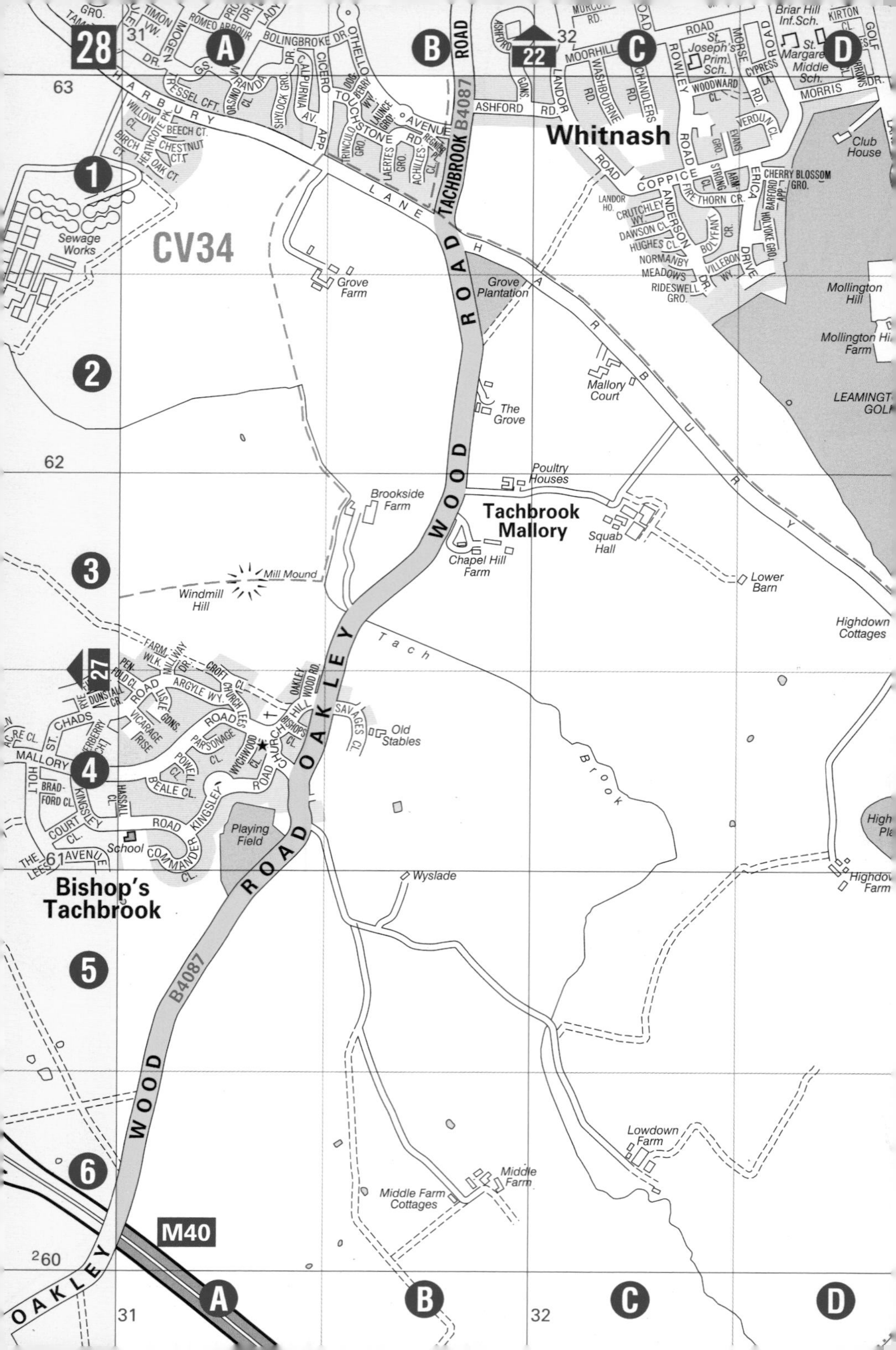

28
22
27
Whitnash
Tachbrook Mallory
Bishop's Tachbrook
CV34
Sewage Works
Grove Farm
Grove Plantation
Mallory Court
The Grove
Poultry Houses
Brookside Farm
Chapel Hill Farm
Squab Hall
Lower Barn
Highdown Cottages
Mill Mound
Windmill Hill
Old Stables
Playing Field
School
Wyslade
Lowdown Farm
Middle Farm
Middle Farm Cottages
Highdown Farm
Mollington Hill
Mollington Hill Farm
Club House
Briar Hill Inf.Sch.
St. Joseph's Prim. Sch.
St. Margaret's Middle Sch.
HARBURY LANE
TACHBROOK ROAD
OAKLEY WOOD ROAD
B4087
M40
Tach Brook
A
B
C
D
1
2
3
4
5
6
31
32
63
62
61
260

E
F
23
34
G
H
435
63
The Meadow
Isle of Wight Barn
Crown Hill
1
Pounces Hill Farm
CV31
2
LANE
Lower Fosse Farm
Frizmore Hill
62
3
WAY
Tropical Bird Garden
Depot
Leamington Hall Farm
4
Bridle Farm
CV33
Hobson's Choice
61
MIDDLE
ROAD
B4455
WARWICK
STRATFORD-ON-AVON
5
Field Barn
LANE
Tach Brook
Whitnash Bushes
Harbury Fields
6
FOSSE
260
E
F
G
H
34
435

INDEX

Including Streets, Places & Areas, Industrial Estates, Selected Subsidiary Addresses and Selected Places of Interest.

HOW TO USE THIS INDEX

1. Each street name is followed by its Posttown or Postal Locality and then by its map reference; e.g. Acacia Rd. *Lea S*—6H **15** is in the Leamington Spa Posttown and is to be found in square 6H on page **15**. The page number being shown in bold type.
   A strict alphabetical order is followed in which Av., Rd., St., etc. (though abbreviated) are read in full and as part of the street name; e.g. Ash Gro. appears after Ashford Rd. but before Ashgrove Pl.

2. Streets and a selection of Subsidiary names not shown on the Maps, appear in the index in *Italics* with the thoroughfare to which it is connected shown in brackets; e.g. *Victoria Colonade. Lea S —2B **22** (off Victoria Ter.)*

3. Places and areas are shown in the index in **bold type**, the map reference referring to the actual map square in which the town or area is located and not to the place name; e.g. **Alveston. —4G 7**

4. An example of a selected place of interest is Anne Hathaway's Cottage. —1E 9

5. Map references shown in brackets; e.g. Albany Rd. *S Avon*—1H **9** (5A **2**) refer to entries that also appear on the large scale pages 2 & 3.

GENERAL ABBREVIATIONS

All : Alley
App : Approach
Arc : Arcade
Av : Avenue
Bk : Back
Boulevd : Boulevard
Bri : Bridge
B'way : Broadway
Bldgs : Buildings
Bus : Business
Cvn : Caravan
Cen : Centre
Chu : Church
Chyd : Churchyard
Circ : Circle
Cir : Circus
Clo : Close
Comn : Common
Cotts : Cottages
Ct : Court
Cres : Crescent
Cft : Croft
Dri : Drive
E : East
Embkmt : Embankment
Est : Estate
Fld : Field
Gdns : Gardens
Gth : Garth
Ga : Gate
Gt : Great
Grn : Green
Gro : Grove
Ho : House
Ind : Industrial
Info : Information
Junct : Junction
La : Lane
Lit : Little
Lwr : Lower
Mc : Mac
Mnr : Manor
Mans : Mansions
Mkt : Market
Mdw : Meadow
M : Mews
Mt : Mount
Mus : Museum
N : North
Pal : Palace
Pde : Parade
Pk : Park
Pas : Passage
Pl : Place
Quad : Quadrant
Res : Residential
Ri : Rise
Rd : Road
Shop : Shopping
S : South
Sq : Square
Sta : Station
St : Street
Ter : Terrace
Trad : Trading
Up : Upper
Va : Vale
Vw : View
Vs : Villas
Vis : Visitors
Wlk : Walk
W : West
Yd : Yard

POSTTOWN AND POSTAL LOCALITY ABBREVIATIONS

A'ton : Alveston
Avon I : Avon Ind. Est.
Barf : Barford
Beau : Beausale
Bis T : Bishops Tachbrook
B'ton : Bishopton
B'dwn : Blackdown
B Hill : Black Hill
Bud : Budbrooke
Char : Charlecote
Ches : Chesterton
Cliff C : Clifford Chambers
Cubb : Cubbington
D'wll : Dodwell
Guys C : Guys Cliffe
H Lucy : Hampton Lucy
H Mag : Hampton Magna
H Hill : Hampton-on-the-Hill
Hase : Haseley
Hatt : Hatton
Hatt P : Hatton Park
H'cte : Heathcote
H'cte I : Heathcote Ind. Est.
Ken : Kenilworth
Lea S : Leamington Spa
Leek W : Leek Wootton
Lill : Lillington
Lwr N : Lower Norton
Ludd : Luddington
N Lin : Norton Lindsey
Off : Offchurch
Old T : Old Town
Rad S : Radford Semele
Sher : Sherbourne
Shot : Shottery
Snitt : Snitterfield
S'lgh : Stoneleigh
S Avon : Stratford-upon-Avon
Syd : Sydenham
Tach P : Tachbrook Park
Tidd : Tiddington
Warw : Warwick
W Avon : Weston on Avon
W Weth : Weston under Wetherley
W'nsh : Whitnash
Wilm : Wilmcote
Wood P : Woodloes Park

INDEX

Abbots Way. *Warw*—3B **20**
Abbotts St. *Lea S*—2B **22**
Acacia Rd. *Lea S*—6H **15**
Achilles Clo. *H'cte*—1B **28**
Acorn Ct. *Lea S*—5C **16**
Acre Clo. *W'nsh*—5C **22**
Addingham Clo. *Warw* —6C **14**
Adelaide Rd. *Lea S*—1A **22**
Adrians Ct. *S Avon*—5A **6**
Aintree Dri. *Lea S*—4E **17**
Aintree Rd. *S Avon*—2F **9**
Albany Rd. *S Avon* —1H **9** (5A **2**)
Albany Ter. *Lea S*—6A **16**
Albert Bean Clo. *W'nsh* —5C **22**
Albert St. *Lea S*—6G **15**
Albert St. *Warw*—2B **20**
Albert Ter. *S Avon*—2E **3**
Alcester Rd. *S Avon* —5A **4** (3A **2**)
Alderminster Gro. *Hatt P* —5E **13**

Alders Rd. *Warw* —5B **20**
Alderton M. *Lea S* —3E **23**
Aldwick Clo. *Lea S* —3C **16**
Alexandra Rd. *Lea S* —3C **22**
Allibone Clo. *W'nsh* —5C **22**
All Saints Rd. *Warw* —6E **15**
Almond Av. *Lea S* —3B **16**
Almond Gro. *Warw* —6E **15**
Almshouses. *S Avon* —1A **10**
Althorpe St. *Lea S* —2C **22**
Alveston. —4G 7
Alveston Hill. —2F 11
Alveston La. *A'ton* —4F **7**
Alveston Leys. *A'ton* —3G **7**
Alveston Pastures Cotts. *A'ton* —2H **11**
Alveston Pl. *Lea S* —6C **16**
Ambassador Ct. *Lea S* —4B **16**
American Fountain. —3C 2
Amherst Bus. Cen. *Warw* —2H **19**
Amroth M. *Lea S* —3E **23**
Anderson Dri. *W'nsh* —1C **28**
Anfield Ct. *Lea S* —2D **22**
Anne Hathaway's Cottage. —1E 9
Ansell Way. *Warw* —2B **20**
Antelope Gdns. *Warw* —1A **20**
Antony Gardner Cres. *W'nsh* —5C **22**
Apollo Way. *Warw* —4H **21**
Approach, The. *Lea S* —3B **22**
Aragon Dri. *Warw* —3G **21**
Arbury Clo. *Lea S* —4C **16**
Archery Fields. *Warw* —3D **20**
Archery Rd. *Lea S* —1A **22**
Arden Clo. *Lea S* —4D **22**
Arden Clo. *Warw* —6E **15**
Arden Clo. *Wilm* —1A **4**
Arden St. *S Avon* —6H **5** (3A **2**)
Argyle Way. *Bis T* —4A **28**
Arley M. *Lea S* —6A **16**
Arlington Av. *Lea S* —5B **16**
Arlington Ct. *Lea S* —5B **16**
Arlington M. *Lea S* —5B **16**
Armscote Gro. *Hatt P* —5D **12**
Armstrong Clo. *Lea S* —1C **28**
Arncliffe Way. *Warw* —6D **14**
Arras Boulevd. *H Mag* —2G **19**
Artemis Dri. *Tach P* —4H **21**
Arthur Rd. *S Avon* —5H **5**
Arundel Clo. *Warw* —1D **20**
Ascot Clo. *S Avon* —2F **9**
Ascot Ride. *Lea S* —4E **17**
Ashford Gdns. *W'nsh* —6B **22**
Ashford Rd. *W'nsh* —1B **28**
Ash Gro. *S Avon* —4G **5**
Ashgrove Pl. *Lea S* —2C **22**
Ashley Cres. *Warw* —3F **21**
Ashton Ct. *Lea S* —4E **17**
Astley Clo. *Lea S* —5H **15**
Aston Cantlow Rd. *Wilm* —1A **4**
Athena Dri. *Tach P* —4H **21**
Augusta Pl. *Lea S* —1B **22**
Austen Ct. *Cubb* —2G **17**
Austin Edwards Dri. *Warw* —1F **21**
Austwick Clo. *Warw* —6C **14**
Avenue Farm. *S Avon* —5G **5**
Avenue Farm Ind. Est. *S Avon* —5G **5**
Avenue Rd. *Lea S* —2A **22**
Avenue Rd. *S Avon* —6A **6** (1F **3**)
Avenue, The. *B'ton* —4F **5**
Avery Ct. *Warw* —3D **20**
Avonbank. *S Avon* —2G **3**
Avonbank Dri. *S Avon* —4E **9**
Avonbrook Clo. *S Avon* —5F **5**
Avon Cvn. Pk. *S Avon* —4D **6**
Avoncliffe. *Tidd* —4E **7**
Avoncliffe Wlk. *Tidd* —4F **7**
Avon Clo. *Barf* —4A **26**
Avon Ct. *Lea S* —4B **16**
Avon Cres. *S Avon* —2D **10**
Avondale Rd. *Lea S* —3E **17**
Avonfields Clo. *A'ton* —4H **7**
Avon Ho. *S Avon* —1D **2**
Avonhurst. *Tidd* —5D **6**
Avonlea Ri. *Lea S* —5H **15**
Avon Mdw. Clo. *S Avon* —2H **9**
Avon Mill. *S Avon* —1E **3**
Avon Rd. *W'nsh* —6C **22**
Avonside. *S Avon* —2A **10**
Avon St. *Warw* —2E **21**
Aylesford St. *Lea S* —3C **22**

Back La. *Warw* —3C **20**
Baddesley Clo. *Syd* —4F **23**
Bagot Way. *H'cte* —6A **22**
Baker Av. *Lea S* —3B **22**
Baker Av. *S Avon* —6F **5**
Balmoral Way. *Lea S* —1E **17**
Bamburgh Gro. *Lea S* —4A **16**
Banbury Rd. *S Avon* —1B **10**
Banbury Rd. *Warw & Bis T* —3D **20**
Banbury Rd. Hill. *Warw* —4E **21**
Bancroft Pl. *S Avon* —6A **6** (3G **3**)
Bankcroft. *Lea S* —4E **23**
Bankfield Dri. *Lea S* —6G **15**
Barber Wlk. *H Mag* —2F **19**
Barcherston Dri. *Hatt P* —4D **12**
Bard's Wlk. *S Avon* —6A **6** (3D **2**)
Barford. —4A 26
Barford App. *W'nsh* —1D **28**
Barley Ct. *Lea S* —5B **16**
Barnack Dri. *Warw* —6C **14**
Barnard Clo. *Lea S* —4E **17**
Barn Clo. *Cliff C* —6H **9**
Barn Clo. *W'nsh* —6D **22**
Barrack St. *Warw* —2C **20**
Bartlett Clo. *Warw* —2D **20**
Barton Cres. *Lea S* —3E **23**
Barwell Clo. *Lea S* —4B **16**
Basant Clo. *Warw* —2E **21**
Bath Pl. *Lea S* —2B **22**
Bath St. *Lea S* —2B **22**
Baxter Ct. *Lea S* —2C **22**
Beaconsfield St. *Lea S* —2D **22**
Beaconsfield St. W. *Lea S* —1D **22**
Beale Clo. *Bis T* —4A **28**
Beauchamp Av. *Lea S* —6B **16**
Beauchamp Ct. *Lea S* —6B **16**
Beauchamp Gdns. *Warw* —3F **21**
Beauchamp Hill. *Lea S* —6A **16**
Beauchamp Rd. *Lea S* —6B **16**
Beauchamp Rd. *Warw* —1F **21**
Beaufell Clo. *Warw* —6C **14**
Beaufort Av. *Lea S* —2E **17**
Beaulieu Pk. *Syd* —3F **23**
Beausale La. *Beau* —1C **12**
Bedford Pl. *Lea S* —1B **22**
Bedford St. *Lea S* —1B **22**
Beecham Wlk. *S Avon* —5E **5**
Beech Cliffe. *Warw* —1D **20**
Beech Clo. *S Avon* —1C **10**
Beech Ct. *H'cte* —1A **28**
Beeches Wlk. *Tidd* —5E **7**
Beech Gro. *Warw* —6F **15**
Bellam Rd. *H Mag* —2F **19**
Bell Ct. *Lea S* —5B **16**
Bell Ct. *S Avon* —4D **2**
Bell Ct. Shop. Cen. *S Avon* —1A **10** (4D **2**)
Bell La. *Shot* —1F **9**
Belmont Ct. *Lea S* —3C **16**
Belmont Dri. *Lea S* —3C **16**
Bennett Dri. *Warw* —2F **21**
Benson Rd. *S Avon* —5A **6**
Bentley Clo. *Lea S* —4D **16**
Berenska Dri. *Lea S* —5C **16**
Berrington Rd. *Lea S* —3D **22**
Bertie Ter. *Lea S* —6A **16**
Berwick Clo. *Warw* —5C **14**
Beverley Rd. *Lea S* —6H **15**
Billesley Rd. *Wilm* —2A **4**
Binswood Av. *Lea S* —5B **16**
Binswood Cres. *Lea S* —5B **16**
Binswood Mans. *Lea S* —5B **16**
Binswood St. *Lea S* —6A **16**
Birch Ct. *H'cte* —1A **28**
Birchfield Rd. *S Avon* —4A **6**
Birchway Clo. *Lea S* —6G **15**
Bird Rd. *H'cte* —5G **21**
Birmingham Rd. *B'ton* —1E **5** (1C **2**)
Birmingham Rd. *Bud* —6G **13**
Birmingham Rd. *Hase & Hatt* —1A **12**
Birmingham Rd. *Warw* —1H **19**
Bishop's Clo. *Bis T* —4A **28**
Bishops Clo. *S Avon* —5E **5**
Bishop's Tachbrook. —4H 27
Bishopton. —3F 5
Bishopton Hill. *B'ton* —1F **5**
Bishopton La. *S Avon* —5D **4**
Bisset Cres. *Lea S* —3E **23**
Blackdown. —2B 16
Black La. *Lea S* —5D **16**
Blacklow Rd. *Warw* —6E **15**
Blackthorn Rd. *S Avon* —4A **6**
Blacon Way. *S Avon* —6E **5**
Bladon Wlk. *Lea S* —3E **23**
Blakelands Av. *Lea S* —3D **22**
Blandford Rd. *Lea S* —6G **15**
Blandford Way. *H Mag* —2G **19**
Blenheim Cres. *Lea S* —4E **23**
Blick Rd. *H'cte I* —5G **21**
Blue Cap Rd. *S Avon* —4A **6**
Boddington Clo. *Lea S* —2G **17**
Boleyn Clo. *Warw* —3G **21**
Bolingbroke Dri. *H'cte* —6A **22**
Bolyfant Cres. *W'nsh* —1C **28**
Bonniksen Clo. *Lea S* —4B **22**
Bordesley Ct. *Lea S* —4C **16**
Bordon Hill. *S Avon* —2E **9**
Bordon Pl. *S Avon* —2G **9**
Borrowdale Dri. *Lea S* —5H **15**
Boswell Gro. *Warw* —6B **14**
Boucher Clo. *S Avon* —2F **9**
Boundary La. *S Avon* —1F **11**
Bourton Dri. *Lea S* —4D **22**
Bowers Cft. *Lea S* —3C **16**
Bowling Grn. St. *Warw* —3B **20**
Box Clo. *W'nsh* —6D **22**
Braemar Rd. *Lea S* —3D **16**
Brakesmead. *Lea S* —4B **22**
Brandon Pde. *Lea S* —1C **22**
Brese Av. *Warw* —6D **14**
Brewery St. *S Avon* —6H **5** (1C **2**)
Briar Clo. *Lea S* —5D **16**
Briar Cft. *S Avon* —1H **9** (3A **2**)
Bridge End. —4D 20

Bridge End. *Warw* —3D **20**
Bridge Foot. *S Avon* —6A **6** (3F **3**)
Bridgefoot Quay. *S Avon* —6A **6** (3G **3**)
Bridge St. *Barf* —5H **25**
Bridge St. *S Avon* —1A **10** (3E **3**)
Bridge St. *Warw* —1F **21**
Bridge Town. —2B 10
Bridgetown Rd. *S Avon* —2B **10**
Bridgeway. *S Avon* —6A **6** (2G **3**)
Broadhaven Clo. *Lea S* —2E **23**
Broadmeadow La. *S Avon* —5E **5**
Broad Oak Ct. *Lea S* —5C **16**
Broad St. *S Avon* —1H **9** (6B **2**)
Broad St. *Warw* —2D **20**
Broad Wlk. *S Avon* —1H **9**
Broadway. *Lea S* —2G **17**
Bromford Way. *S Avon* —5F **5**
Brooke Clo. *Warw* —4D **20**
Brookfield Rd. *Lea S* —2G **17**
Brook House. —6E 3
Brookhurst Ct. *Lea S* —6H **15**
Brookside Clo. *S Avon* —6F **5**
Brookside Rd. *S Avon* —6F **5**
Brook St. *Warw* —3C **20**
Brookvale Rd. *S Avon* —1G **9**
Browning Av. *Warw* —4A **20**
Brownlow Green. —3D 12
Brownlow St. *Lea S* —5C **16**
Broxell Clo. *Warw* —6A **14**
Broxell Clo. Ind. Est. *Warw* —6A **14**
Brunel Clo. *W'nsh* —6D **22**
Brunswick Ct. *Lea S* —4C **22**
Brunswick St. *Lea S* —3C **22**
Buckden Clo. *Warw* —6D **14**
Buckley Rd. *Lea S* —5D **16**
Budbrooke. —2F 19
Budbrooke Ind. Est. *Warw* —2A **20**
Budbrooke Rd. *Warw* —2H **19**
Bull St. *S Avon* —2H **9**
Burbage Av. *S Avon* —4H **5**
Burbury Clo. *Lea S* —5E **17**
Burbury Ct. *Warw* —1F **21**
Burford M. *Lea S* —3E **23**
Burford Rd. *S Avon* —1D **10**
Burges Gro. *Warw* —6D **14**
Burns Av. *Warw* —4A **20**
Burnside Rd. *Shot* —1E **9**
Burns Rd. *Lea S* —3D **16**
Burrows Clo. *W'nsh* —6D **22**
Bury Rd. *Lea S* —2A **22**
Butts, The. *Warw* —2C **20**
Byron Av. *Warw* —5A **20**
Byron Rd. *S Avon* —2B **10**

Caen Clo. *H Mag* —2G **19**
Calder Wlk. *Lea S* —3E **23**
Calpurnia Av. *H'cte* —6A **22**
Camberwell Ter. *Lea S* —2C **22**
Cambridge Gdns. *Lea S* —6C **16**
Cameron Clo. *Lea S* —3C **16**
Campden Rd. *Cliff C* —6G **9**
Campion Ct. *Lea S* —5C **16**
Campion Grn. *Lea S* —5C **16**
Campion Rd. *Lea S* —5C **16**
Campion Ter. *Lea S* —6C **16**
Canada La. *N Lin* —1A **24**
Canal La. *Hatt* —5C **12**
Canon Young Rd. *W'nsh* —5D **22**
Cape Ind. Est. *Warw* —2C **20**
Cape Rd. *Warw* —1B **20**
Cape, The. —1B 20
Capulet Dri. *H'cte* —6A **22**
Carew Clo. *S Avon* —4G **5**
Carter Dri. *Barf* —5H **25**
Carters La. *Tidd* —4E **7**
Cashmore Av. *Lea S* —4B **22**
Cassandra Gro. *H'cte* —5H **21**
Castle Clo. *Warw* —3C **20**
Castle Ct. *Warw* —3C **20**
Castle Ga. M. *Warw* —2D **20**
Castle Hill. *Warw* —3C **20**
Castle La. *Warw* —3C **20**
Castle St. *Warw* —3C **20**
Caswell Rd. *Lea S* —3D **22**
Cattell Rd. *Warw* —2C **20**
Cedar Clo. *Lea S* —3C **16**
Cedar Clo. *S Avon* —5B **6**
Cedar Gro. *Warw* —6E **15**
Cedars, The. *Lea S* —1H **21**
Central Av. *Lea S* —3B **22**
Central Chambers. *S Avon* —3D **2**
Cen. Craft Yd. *S Avon* —3D **2**
Chamberlain Clo. *Cubb* —2F **17**
Chance Fields. *Rad S* —3H **23**
Chanders Rd. *Warw* —6B **14**
Chandlers Rd. *W'nsh* —6C **22**
Chandos St. *Lea S* —6B **16**
Chantry, The. *Warw* —6E **15**
Chapel Ct. *Lea S* —1C **22**
Chapel La. *S Avon* —1A **10** (6D **2**)
Chapel Row. *Warw* —2C **20**
Chapel St. *Lea S* —2C **22**
Chapel St. *S Avon* —1A **10** (5D **2**)
Chapel St. *Warw* —2C **20**
Chapman Clo. *Rad S* —4G **23**
Chapman Ct. *Warw* —1G **21**
Charingworth Dri. *Hatt P* —5E **13**
Charlbury M. *Lea S* —3E **23**
Charlcote Clo. *Tidd* —6E **7**
Charlecote Gdns. *Syd* —4F **23**
Charles Ct. *Warw* —1F **21**
Charles Gardner Rd. *Lea S* —3C **22**
Charles St. *Warw* —1E **21**
Charles Watson Ct. *Lea S* —5C **16**
Charlotte St. *Lea S* —3B **22**
Charnwood Way. *Lea S* —4E **17**
Charter App. *Warw* —4B **20**
Chatsworth Gdns. *Syd* —3F **23**
Chepstow Clo. *S Avon* —2G **9**
Cherry Blossom Gro. *W'nsh* —1D **28**
Cherry La. *H Mag* —3F **19**
Cherry Orchard. *S Avon* —2G **9**
Cherry St. *S Avon* —2H **9**
Cherry St. *Warw* —2D **20**
Chesford Cres. *Warw* —6F **15**
Chesford Gro. *S Avon* —5F **5**
Chesham St. *Lea S* —2D **22**
Chesterton Dri. *Lea S* —4E **23**
Chestnut Ct. *H'cte* —1A **28**
Chestnut Sq. *Lea S* —5D **16**
Chestnut Wlk. *S Avon* —1H **9** (6B **2**)
Cheviot Ri. *Lea S* —4E **17**
Chichester La. *H Mag* —3F **19**
Childs Clo. *S Avon* —4G **5**
Christine Ledger Sq. *Lea S* —3C **22**
Church Clo. *Ludd* —5B **8**
Church Clo. *W'nsh* —5D **22**
Church End. *Rad S* —3G **23**
Church Hill. *Bis T* —4A **28**
Church Hill. *Cubb* —2G **17**
Church Hill. *Lea S* —1A **22**
Church La. *A'ton* —4G **7**
Church La. *Barf* —5A **26**
Church La. *Cubb* —1G **17**
Church La. *Lea S* —4C **16**
Church La. *N Lin* —6A **18**
Church La. *Shot* —6E **5**
Church La. *W'nsh* —5D **22**
Church Lees. *Bis T* —4A **28**
Church Path. *H Mag* —3F **19**
Church Rd. *Sher* —3G **25**
Church Rd. *Wilm* —1A **4**
Church St. *Barf* —5H **25**
Church St. *Lea S* —2C **22**
Church St. *S Avon* —1H **9** (6C **2**)
Church St. *Warw* —3C **20**
Church Ter. *Cubb* —2G **17**
Church Ter. *Lea S* —2C **22**
Church Wlk. *Lea S* —2B **22**
Cicero App. *H'cte* —6A **22**
Circuit, The. *D'wll* —3B **8**
Clapham Sq. *Lea S* —2D **22**
Clapham St. *Lea S* —3D **22**
Clapham Ter. *Lea S* —2D **22**
Clare Clo. *Lea S* —5E **17**
Claremont Rd. *Lea S* —3B **22**
Clarence Rd. *S Avon* —6F **5**
Clarence St. *Lea S* —3C **22**
Clarence Ter. *Lea S* —6B **16**
Clarendon Av. *Lea S* —6B **16**
Clarendon Cres. *Lea S* —6A **16**
Clarendon Pl. *Lea S* —6A **16**
Clarendon Sq. *Lea S* (in two parts) —6A **16**
Clarendon St. *Lea S* —6C **16**
Clarkson Dri. *W'nsh* —5C **22**
Cleeves Av. *Warw* —3G **21**
Clemens St. *Lea S* —2C **22**
Cleveland Ct. *Lea S* —5B **16**
Cliffe Ct. *Lea S* —6H **15**
Cliffe Rd. *Lea S* —6H **15**
Cliffe Way. *Warw* —1D **20**
Clifford Chambers. —6G 9
Clifford La. *Cliff C* —5H **9**
Clinton Av. *H Mag* —2G **19**
Clinton St. *Lea S* —2C **22**
Cloister Crofts. *Lea S* —4B **16**
Cloisters, The. *Lea S* —4B **16**
Cloister Way. *Lea S* —4B **16**
Clopton. —4A 6
Clopton Bridge. —5H 3 (5H 3)
Clopton Ct. *S Avon* —6H **5** (1C **2**)
Clopton Rd. *S Avon* —6H **5** (1C **2**)
Close, The. *Lea S* —3C **22**
Clover Clo. *S Avon* —4G **5**
Cobden Av. *Lea S* —4E **23**
Cobham Grn. *W'nsh* —5B **22**
Cockermouth Clo. *Lea S* —5H **15**
Cocksfoot Clo. *S Avon* —4G **5**
Cocksparrow St. *Warw* —3B **20**
Colbourne Gro. *Lea S* —5H **15**
College Dri. *Lea S* —5B **16**
College La. *S Avon* —2H **9**
College M. *S Avon* —2H **9**
College St. *S Avon* —2H **9**
Collegiate Church of St Mary. —3C 20
Collins Rd. *H'cte I* —4H **21**
Combroke Gro. *Hatt P* —5E **13**
Commainge Clo. *Warw* —2B **20**
Commander Clo. *Bis T* —4A **28**
Compton Clo. *Lea S* —5E **17**
Comyn St. *Lea S* —6D **16**
Congreve Clo. *Warw* —5D **14**
Conifer Gro. *Lea S* —4C **22**

Coningsby Clo. *Lea S* —3E **23**
Coniston Rd. *Lea S* —6H **15**
Conrad Ho. *S Avon* —1C **2**
Conway Rd. *Lea S* —1H **21**
Cooke Clo. *Warw* —6D **14**
Cook's All. *S Avon* —3D **2**
Coppice Clo. *S Avon* —4A **6**
Coppice Rd. *W'nsh* —6D **22**
Copps Rd. *Lea S* —1H **21**
Corbison Clo. *Warw* —6B **14**
Cordelia Grn. *H'cte* —5A **22**
Cornwall Clo. *Warw* —6D **14**
Cornwall Pl. *Lea S* —6H **15**
Corston M. *Lea S* —3E **23**
Cosford Clo. *Lea S* —4D **16**
Coten End. *Warw* —2D **20**
Cottage Clo. *Lea S* —3E **23**
Cottage La. *Shot* —1E **9**
Cotterills Clo. *W'nsh* —6D **22**
Cotton Mill Spinney. *Cubb* —1G **17**
Coughton Dri. *Syd* —4F **23**
Court Clo. *Bis T* —4H **27**
Court St. *Lea S* —2C **22**
Courtyard, The. *Warw* —3D **20**
Coventry Rd. *S'lgh & Cubb* —1G **17**
Coventry Rd. *Warw* —2D **20**
Cowdray Clo. *Lea S* —2E **23**
Cowper Clo. *Warw* —6D **14**
Cox's Orchard. *W'nsh* —5C **22**
Crabtree Gro. *Lea S* —3E **23**
Craig Clo. *Lea S* —3D **22**
Crane Clo. *S Avon* —4E **5**
Crane Clo. *Warw* —6B **14**
Cranmer Gro. *H'cte* —6H **21**
Crawford Clo. *Lea S* —2D **16**
Crest, The. *Lea S* —4E **17**
Crimscote Sq. *Hatt P* —4D **12**
Croft Clo. *Bis T* —4A **28**
Croft Clo. *Warw* —2G **21**
Croft Rd. *Leek W* —1E **15**
Cromer Rd. *Lea S* —5D **16**
Crompton St. *Warw* —3B **20**
Crossfields Rd. *Warw* —1D **20**
Cross La. *Cubb* —3G **17**
Cross Rd. *Lea S* —1H **21**
Cross St. *Lea S* —6C **16**
Cross St. *Warw* —2D **20**
Crown Way. *Lea S* —4D **16**
Crutchley Way. *W'nsh* —1C **28**
Cubbington. —2G 17
Cubbington Rd. *Lea S* —4C **16**
Culworth Clo. *Lea S* —4B **22**
Culworth Ct. *Lea S* —4C **22**
Cumberland Cres. *Lea S* —4F **17**
Cumming St. *Lea S* —2C **22**
Cundall Clo. *Lea S* —3D **22**
Curlew Clo. *S Avon* —4E **5**
Curlieu Clo. *H Mag* —2G **19**
Curran Clo. *W'nsh* —5D **22**
Curzon Gro. *Lea S* —3E **23**
Cypress La. *W'nsh* —6D **22**

Dale Av. *S Avon* —2C **10**
Dale Clo. *Warw* —1E **21**
Dale St. *Lea S* —1A **22**
Daly Av. *H Mag* —3F **19**
Damson Rd. *H Mag* —3F **19**
Danesbury Cres. *Lea S* —3F **23**
Dark La. *Hatt* —6A **12**
Dark La. *Tidd* —5E **7**
Davidson Av. *Lea S* —2C **22**
Davis Clo. *Lea S* —5H **15**
Dawson Clo. *W'nsh* —1C **28**
Deansway. *Warw* —5B **14**
Deerpark Dri. *Warw* —1C **20**
Delamere Way. *Lea S* —3E **17**
Delphi Clo. *Tach P* —5A **22**
Denby Clo. *Lea S* —5E **17**
Denne Clo. *S Avon* —4A **6**
Dennett Clo. *Warw* —5D **14**
Denville Rd. *Lea S* —4C **16**
Dereham Ct. *Lea S* —5C **16**
Derwent Clo. *Lea S* —6H **15**
Dickins Rd. *Warw* —1F **21**
Dighton Clo. *Cliff C* —6H **9**
Dingles Way. *S Avon* —4A **6**
Dobson La. *W'nsh* —5C **22**
Dodd Av. *Warw* —2G **21**
Dodwell Trailer Pk. *D'wll* —3B **8**
Dogberry Way. *H'cte* —1B **28**
Doglands, The. *Lea S* —5D **22**
Dongan Rd. *Warw* —2C **20**
Dorchester Av. *H Mag* —3F **19**
Dormer Pl. *Lea S* —1B **22**
Dorsington Clo. *Hatt P* —4E **13**
Drayton. —6B 4
Drayton Av. *S Avon* —5E **5**
Drayton Clo. *S Avon* —5F **5**
Drayton Ct. *Warw* —5D **14**
Drayton Mnr. Dri. *S Avon* —1B **8**
Dudley Grn. *Lea S* —5D **16**
Dugard Pl. *Barf* —6A **26**
Dugdale Av. *S Avon* —4A **6**
Dugdale Ct. *Lea S* —3C **22**
Duke St. *Lea S* —6C **16**
Dunblane Dri. *Lea S* —2E **17**
Dunstall Cres. *Bis T* —4H **27**
Dwarris Wlk. *Warw* —5C **14**

Eagle St. *Lea S* —3C **22**
Earl Rivers Av. *H'cte* —6H **21**
Earl St. *Lea S* —6C **16**
East Dene. *Lea S* —5D **16**
Eastfield Clo. *S Avon* —4H **5**
Eastfield Rd. *Lea S* —1C **22**
Eastgate M. *Warw* —3C **20**
E. Green Dri. *S Avon* —6E **5**
East Gro. *Lea S* —3C **22**
Eastley Cres. *Warw* —1H **19**
Eastnor Gro. *Lea S* —2D **22**
Eastwood Clo. *Lea S* —3F **23**
Eaton Clo. *Lea S* —5H **15**
Eborall Clo. *Warw* —5C **14**
Ebrington Dri. *Hatt P* —5E **13**
Eden Ct. *Lea S* —4F **17**
Edinburgh Cres. *Lea S* —3B **22**
Edmondes Clo. *Warw* —6D **14**
Edmondscote Rd. *Lea S* —1G **21**
Edward St. *Lea S* —6G **15**
Edward St. *Warw* —2B **20**
Elan Clo. *Lea S* —4E **17**
Eliot Clo. *Warw* —5C **14**
Elizabeth Ct. *Warw* —3F **21**
Elizabeth Pl. *S Avon* —1B **2**
Elizabeth Rd. *Lea S* —3A **22**
Elliotts Orchard. *Barf* —5H **25**
Elliston Gro. *Lea S* —3E **23**
Elm Bank Clo. *Lea S* —3C **16**
Elm Ct. *S Avon* —2B **2**
Elm Rd. *Lea S* —4D **16**
Elm Rd. *S Avon* —4H **5**
Elms Cvn. Pk., The. *S Avon* —4D **6**
Elms, The. *Leek W* —1D **14**
Elms, The. *S Avon* —5A **6**
Elsinore. *S Avon* —1E **3**
Elton Clo. *Lea S* —5E **17**
Ely Cotts. *S Avon* —5D **2**
Ely Gdns. *S Avon* —5C **2**
Ely St. *S Avon* —1H **9** (4C **2**)
Emerald Way. *Lea S* —4B **22**
Emmott Dri. *Lea S* —3D **22**
Emscote. —2E 21
Emscote Rd. *Warw* —2E **21**
Endsleigh Gdns. *Lea S* —3D **22**
England Cres. *Lea S* —2A **22**
Ennerdale Clo. *Lea S* —5H **15**
Enright Clo. *Lea S* —5A **16**
Epperston Ct. *Lea S* —2B **22**
Epping Way. *Lea S* —3E **17**
Epsom Rd. *Lea S* —3E **17**
Erica Dri. *W'nsh* —1D **28**
Essex Ct. *Warw* —1C **20**
Eton Rd. *S Avon* —2C **10**
Europa Way. *Warw* —5G **21**
Euston Pl. *Lea S* —1B **22**
Euston Sq. *Lea S* —1B **22**
Evans Clo. *S Avon* —2F **9**
Evans Gro. *W'nsh* —1C **28**
Evenlode Clo. *S Avon* —2C **10**
Evesham Pl. *S Avon* —1H **9** (6A **2**)
Evesham Rd. *D'wll* —3A **8** (in two parts)
Exhall Clo. *S Avon* —2D **10**
Exham Clo. *Warw* —6C **14**
Exmoor Dri. *Lea S* —3E **17**
Eyffler Dri. *Warw* —2B **20**

Fairfax Clo. *Barf* —5H **25**
Fairfax Ct. *Warw* —2D **20**
Fairfields Wlk. *S Avon* —6F **5**
Fairhurst Dri. *Lea S* —4A **16**
Fairlawn Clo. *Lea S* —6H **15**
Fairways, The. *Lea S* —5H **15**
Fallow Hill. *Lea S* —3E **23**
Falstaff Ct. *S Avon* —6A **6** (2D **2**)
Falstaff Gro. *H'cte* —6A **22**
Farley St. *Lea S* —2D **22**
Farm Rd. *Lea S* —4D **16**
Farm Wlk. *Bis T* —3A **28**
Faulconbridge Way. *H'cte* —6A **22**
Fell Gro. *Lea S* —4E **17**
Fellmore Gro. *Lea S* —2E **23**
Fernhill Dri. *Lea S* —6D **16**
Ferry La. *A'ton* —3H **7**
Fetherston Ct. *Lea S* —3B **22**
Fld. Barn Rd. *H Mag* —2F **19**
Field Clo. *Warw* —2F **21**
Fieldgate La. *W'nsh* —1D **28**
Fieldhead La. *Warw* —3F **21**
Fields Ct. *Warw* —1D **20**
Finings Ct. *Lea S* —5B **16**
Firethorn Cres. *W'nsh* —1C **28**
Fishers Ct. *Warw* —5B **20**
Flavel Cres. *Lea S* —2B **22**
Fleur-de-Lys Ct. *Warw* —1F **21**
Flower Ct. *S Avon* —2H **9**
Flower Rd. *S Avon* —3H **5**
Fordham Av. *S Avon* —5A **6**
Forfield Pl. *Lea S* —2C **22**
Fosberry Clo. *Warw* —1F **21**
Fosse Way. *Ches & Rad S* —6G **29**
Fountain Way. *S Avon* —1H **9** (4D **2**)
Foxdale Wlk. *Lea S* —3E **23**
Foxes La. *Wilm* —1A **4**
Foxes Way. *Warw* —5B **20**
Foxtail Clo. *S Avon* —4F **5**
Frances Av. *Warw* —2E **21**
Frances Gibbs Gdns. *W'nsh* —5C **22**
Frances Havergal Clo. *Lea S* —3B **22**
Frankel Gdns. *Warw* —6D **14**
Franklin Rd. *W'nsh* —6C **22**
Freemans Clo. *Lea S* —6A **16**
Freshwater Gro. *Lea S* —3E **23**
Friars St. *Warw* —3B **20**
Friary Clo. *H Mag* —3E **19**

Fryer Av. Lea S —5A 16
Fulbrook La. Sher —5E 25

Gadshill. H'cte —5A 22
Gainsborough Dri. Lea S —3E 23
Gainsborough Dri. S. Lea S —3D 22
Gainsborough Rd. S Avon —2F 9
Gallows Hill. Warw —4E 21
Garden Ct. Warw —1G 21
Garden Row. S Avon —5C 2
Gardens, The. Rad S —4G 23
Gardens, The. S Avon —1H 9 (5C 2)
Garrick Way. S Avon —2G 9
Garway Clo. Lea S —3C 16
Gas St. Lea S —2B 22
Gaveston Clo. Warw —1D 20
Gaveston Rd. Lea S —6A 16
George Rd. Warw —1E 21
George St. Lea S —2C 22
Gerrard St. Warw —3C 20
Gibbs La. Tidd —5E 7
Giffard Way. Warw —6C 14
Gifford Wlk. S Avon —5E 5
Gilbert Clo. S Avon —3H 5
Ginkgo Wlk. Lea S —4B 22
Girvan Gro. Lea S —2E 17
Gisburn Clo. Warw —6D 14
Gleave Rd. W'nsh —6C 22
Glebe Est. Wilm —1A 4
Glebe Pl. Lea S —2D 22
Glebe Rd. S Avon —5E 5
Gleeson Dri. Warw —6C 14
Glendower. S Avon —1F 3
Glendower App. H'cte —6A 22
Gloucester Ct. S Avon —6A 6 (3E 3)
Gloucester St. Lea S —2C 22
Glover Clo. Warw —5H 19
Godfrey Clo. Rad S —4G 23
Goldacre Clo. W'nsh —5B 22
Goldsmith Av. Warw —4A 20
Golf La. W'nsh —6D 22
Gooch's Way. W'nsh —5C 22
Goodfellow St. Lea S —6G 15
Goodwood Clo. S Avon —2F 9
Gordon Pas. Lea S —2C 22
Gordon St. Lea S —2C 22
Gould Rd. H Mag —2G 19
Gower Memorial, The. —1A 10 (4G 3)
Grammer School & Guildhall. —6D 2
Granborough Ct. Lea S —4C 16
Grange Clo. Warw —1G 21
Grange M., The. Lea S —6H 15
Grange Pk. S Avon —5A 6
Grange Rd. Lea S —4D 16
Grange, The. Cubb —2H 17
Grange, The. Lea S —6D 16
Grange, The. Warw —2F 21
Granleigh Ct. Lea S —2G 17
Granville St. Lea S —5C 16
Grassington Av. Warw —6D 14
Greatheed Rd. Lea S —6A 16
Gt. William St. S Avon —6A 6 (2D 2)
Greaves Clo. Warw —2G 21
Green Clo. W'nsh —5D 22
Greenhill Rd. W'nsh —5D 22
Greenhill St. S Avon —6H 5 (3B 2)
Green La. Warw —1D 20
Green, The. Hatt —4A 12
Green, The. Wilm —1A 4
Greenway. Warw —6C 14
Greenways, The. Lea S —4D 16
Greenwood Ct. Lea S —6D 16
Grenfell Clo. Lea S —3F 23
Gresham Av. Lea S —5D 16
Gresham Pl. Lea S —5D 16
Greswoldes, The. Rad S —3H 23
Greville Rd. Warw —6F 15
Greville Smith Av. W'nsh —5D 22
Griffin Rd. Warw —2G 21
Grosvenor Ct. Lea S —6B 16
Grosvenor Rd. Lea S —4C 22
Grouse Clo. S Avon —4E 5
Grove Cft. H Hill —4E 19
Grove Ho. S Avon —1H 9 (4B 2)
Grove Pl. Lea S —3C 22 (in two parts)
Grove Rd. S Avon —1H 9 (6A 2)
Grove St. Lea S —1A 22
Guild Chapel, The. —6D 2
Guild Cotts., The. Warw —3C 20
Guild St. S Avon —6A 6 (2D 2)
Gulistan Ct. Lea S —6A 16
Gulistan Rd. Lea S —6A 16
Gulliman's Way. Lea S —3F 23
Gundry Clo. Lea S —2C 22
Gunnery Ter. Lea S —6H 15
Guy Pl. E. Lea S —6B 16
Guy Pl. W. Lea S —6B 16
Guy's Cliffe. —4E 15
Guy's Cliffe Av. Lea S —5G 15
Guy's Cliffe House. —5E 15
Guy's Cliffe Rd. Lea S —6H 15
Guy's Cliffe Ter. Warw —2D 20
Guys Clo. Warw —1D 20
Guys Cross Pk. Rd. Warw —1D 20
Guy St. Lea S —6B 16
Guy St. Warw —2D 20

Haddon Rd. Lea S —5D 16
Hadrian Clo. Lea S —3D 16
Halford Rd. S Avon —2G 9
Hallfields. Rad S —4G 23
Hall Rd. Lea S —6B 16
Hall's Clo. W'nsh —6D 22
Halls Croft. —1A 10
Hamilton Rd. Rad S —4G 23
Hamilton Rd. Tidd —6E 7
Hamilton Ter. Lea S —1B 22
Hamlet, The. Leek W —1E 15
Hampton Cft. H Hill —5E 19
Hampton Gro. Lea S —6D 16
Hampton Magna. —3G 19
Hampton on the Hill. —3E 19
Hampton Rd. Warw —4F 19
Hampton St. Warw —3B 20
Handley Gro. Warw —6B 14
Hanover Gdns. Lea S —6C 16
Hanworth Clo. Lea S —4D 16
Hanworth Rd. Warw —1B 20
Harbury La. H'cte —5G 21
Hareway La. Barf —4B 26
Harmar Clo. Warw —6B 14
Harriott Dri. H'cte I —5H 21
Harris Rd. Warw —1A 20
Harrow Rd. W'nsh —6D 22
Harvard House. —1A 10 (4D 2)
Harvest Hill Clo. Lea S —3E 23
Haseley. —3B 12
Haseley Bus. Cen. Hase —3B 12
Haseley Clo. Lea S —4D 22
Hassall Clo. Bis T —4A 28
Hathaway Dri. Warw —5B 14
Hathaway Grn. La. S Avon —6D 4
Hathaway Hamlet. Shot —6E 5
Hathaway La. S Avon —1F 9
Hatherell Rd. Rad S —4G 23
Hatton. —4C 12
Hatton Bank La. B Hill —1H 7
Hatton Clo. Hatt —5E 13
Hatton Country World. —6B 12
Hatton Green. —4A 12
Hatton Hill. —5C 12
Hatton Lock Flight. —5C 12
Hatton Ter. Hatt —5D 12
Hauley Gro. W'nsh —5C 22
Hawkes Dri. H'cte I —5H 21
Hawthorn Rd. Lea S —3B 22
Haydock Clo. S Avon —2G 9
Hayle Av. Warw —6D 14
Hayward Clo. H Mag —3F 19
Hazel Clo. Lea S —5C 16
Healey Ct. Warw —2D 20
Heathcote. —6H 21
Heathcote Ind. Est. H'cte I —5G 21
Heathcote La. H'cte —5G 21
Heathcote Pk. H'cte —1A 28
Heathcote Rd. W'nsh —6B 22
Heathcote Way. H'cte I —5H 21
Heath End. —5A 24
Heath End La. Snitt —4A 24
Heather Clo. S Avon —6F 5
Heath Ter. Lea S —6A 16
Hebden Av. Warw —6C 14
Heemstede La. Lea S —5C 16
Hellidon Clo. Lea S —5C 16
Helmsdale Rd. Lea S —3D 16
Hemmin Gdns. Mill. Barf —5H 25
Hemmings Clo. Rad S —4G 23
Henley Rd. Lea S —4D 22
Henley Rd. Lwr N —4A 18
Henley St. S Avon —6A 6 (2C 2)
Henry Tanday Ct. Lea S —6A 16
Heralds Ct. Warw —1F 21
Hermes Clo. Warw —4A 22
Heron La. S Avon —4E 5
Hertford Rd. S Avon —2H 9
Hetton Clo. Warw —6D 14
Hicks Clo. Warw —5D 14
Hidcote Clo. Syd —4E 23
Highcroft Cres. Lea S —6G 15
Highdown Rd. Lea S —3D 22
Highfield Rd. S Avon —4G 5
Highfield Ter. Lea S —6H 15
Highland Rd. Lea S —3D 16
Highlands Clo. Warw —1D 20
High St. Barf —4A 26
High St. Cubb —2G 17
High St. Lea S —2B 22
High St. S Avon —1A 10 (4E 3)
High St. Warw —3C 20
High Vw. Rd. Lea S —2E 17
Hill Clo. Lea S —4C 16
Hillcrest. Lea S —2G 17
Hillside Rd. S Avon —5E 5
Hill St. Lea S —6C 16
Hill St. Warw —1F 21
Hill Wootton. —1G 15
Hill Wootton Rd. Leek W —1E 15
Hind Clo. Warw —5D 14
Hiron Way. Warw —2H 19
Hirsel Gdns. Lea S —5B 16
Hitchman Ct. Lea S —4C 22
Hitchman M. Lea S —4C 22

Hitchman Rd. *Lea S* —3C **22**
Hockley Rd. *Hatt* —4A **12**
Hodgson Rd. *S Avon* —4H **5**
Hogarth Rd. *S Avon* —2F **9**
Holbrook Rd. *S Avon* —6E **5**
Holioake Dri. *Warw* —3E **21**
Holloway, The. *Warw* —3B **20**
Holly St. *Lea S* —6C **16**
Holly Wlk. *Lea S* —1B **22** (in two parts)
Holly Wlk. *S Avon* —5E **5**
Holmes Rd. *W'nsh* —6D **22**
Holt Av. *Bis T* —4H **27**
Holtom St. *S Avon* —2H **9**
Holt, The. *Lea S* —4D **16**
Holyoke Gro. *W'nsh* —1D **28**
Holy Trinity Church. —2A 10
Home Farm. *Leek W* —1D **14**
Home Farm Cres. *W'nsh* —5D **22**
Homer Clo. *Tach P* —4A **22**
Hopton Crofts. *Lea S* —5G **15**
Hornbeam Gro. *Lea S* —3E **23**
Howard Wlk. *Warw* —3H **21**
Huddisdon Clo. *Warw* —6D **14**
Hughes Clo. *W'nsh* —1C **28**
Hughes Clo. *Wood P* —5B **14**
Hughes, The. *Warw* —3C **20**
Humphris St. *Warw* —1F **21**
Hunscote La. *A'ton & Char* —1G **11**
Hunt Clo. *H Mag* —3F **19**
Hunts Rd. *S Avon* —2B **10**
Hurlbutt Rd. *H'cte I* —5G **21**
Hurley Clo. *Lea S* —5C **16**
Hyde Pl. *Lea S* —1A **22**

Ilex Ct. *Warw* —2E **21**
Ilmington Clo. *Hatt P* —5D **12**
Imogen Gdns. *H'cte* —6A **22**
Inchford Av. *Warw* —5C **14**
Ingle Ct. *Lea S* —2A **22**
Inglewood Clo. *Lea S* —4C **16**
Ingon. —1D 6
Ingon La. *S Avon* —1C **6**
Innage Clo. *Lea S* —1C **22**

Jackson Clo. *H Mag* —3E **19**
James Ct. *Warw* —2D **20**
Jasmine Gro. *Lea S* —5C **16**
Jenton Rd. *Lea S* —3D **22**
Jephson Gardens. —1C 22
Jephson Pl. *Lea S* —2D **22**
Jitty, The. *Warw* —3B **20**
Joans Clo. *Lea S* —3E **23**
John St. *Lea S* —1B **22**
John St. *S Avon* —6A **6** (3E **3**)
Jolyffe Ct. *S Avon* —5H **5**
Jolyffe Pk. Rd. *S Avon* —5H **5**
Joseph Way. *S Avon* —4G **5**
Jourdain Pk. *H'cte* —6A **22**
Joyce Pool. *Warw* —2C **20**
Jubilee Wlk. *Shot* —1F **9**
Judith Quiney's House. —4E 3
Juno Dri. *Lea S* —4B **22**
Jury St. *Warw* —3C **20**
Justice Clo. *W'nsh* —5C **22**
Justins Av. *S Avon* —4G **5**

Keats Rd. *S Avon* —2B **10**
Keir Clo. *Lea S* —5C **16**
Keith Rd. *Lea S* —3D **16**
Kelvin Rd. *Lea S* —2D **16**
Kemp Clo. *Warw* —2E **21**
Kempton Cres. *Lea S* —3E **17**
Kendal Av. *Lea S* —5G **15**
Kendall Av. *S Avon* —6H **5**
Kenilworth By-Pass. *Ken* —2E **15**
Kenilworth Rd. *Cubb* —1E **17**
Kenilworth Rd. *Ken & B'dwn* —1A **16**
Kenilworth St. *Lea S* —6B **16**
Kennan Av. *Lea S* —2B **22**
Kennedy Sq. *Lea S* —6C **16**
Kerns Ter. *S Avon* —6A **6** (1E **3**)
Kestrel Clo. *S Avon* —4A **6**
Keswick Grn. *Lea S* —6H **15**
Kettlewell Clo. *Warw* —6C **14**
Keyte's La. *Barf* —5A **26**
Kilby Gro. *Syd* —4E **23**
Kildwick Way. *Warw* —6C **14**
Kiln Clo. *Lea S* —5C **16**
Kilnsey Gro. *Warw* —6C **14**
Kingfisher Ct. *S Avon* —2E **3**
Kingland Dri. *Lea S* —6G **15**
Kingshurst. *Rad S* —3G **23**
King's La. *S Avon* —2F **5** (in two parts)
Kingsley Rd. *Bis T* —4H **27**
Kingston M. *Lea S* —3E **23**
King St. *Lea S* —6C **16**
Kingsway. *Lea S* —3A **22**
Kinross Rd. *Lea S* —3D **16**
Kipling Av. *Warw* —5A **20**
Kipling Rd. *S Avon* —3B **10**
Kirby Av. *Warw* —6D **14**
Kirton Clo. *W'nsh* —6D **22**
Kissing Tree La. *A'ton* —4G **7**
Kites Clo. *Warw* —5C **14**
Kites Nest La. *Beau* —1D **12**
Knightcote Dri. *Lea S* —1A **22**
Knight Ct. *S Avon* —4C **2**
Knightley Clo. *Lea S* —2G **17**
Knights La. *Tidd* —5E **7**
Knoll Dri. *Warw* —6C **14**

Laburnum Cotts. *S Avon* —1H **9** (4B **2**)
Laburnum Dri. *W'nsh* —6D **22**
Laburnum Gro. *Warw* —6F **15**
Lacell Clo. *Warw* —6B **14**
Ladbroke Pk. *Warw* —6C **14**
Ladycroft. *Lea S* —3G **17**
Lady Grey Av. *H'cte* —6A **22**
Laertes Gro. *H'cte* —1B **28**
Lakeland Ho. *Warw* —2E **21**
Lakin Ct. *Warw* —1D **20**
Lakin Rd. *Warw* —1D **20**
Lambourn Cres. *Lea S* —3E **23**
Lamintone Dri. *Lea S* —4H **15**
Lammas Cft. *W'nsh* —6C **22**
Lammas Wlk. *Warw* —2B **20**
Landor Ho. *W'nsh* —1C **28**
Landor Rd. *Warw* —1B **20**
Landor Rd. *W'nsh* —6C **22**
Langcliffe Av. *Warw* —6D **14**
Langdale Clo. *Lea S* —4F **17**
Langley Rd. *Lea S* —5C **22**
Lansdowne Cir. *Lea S* —6C **16**
Lansdowne Cres. *Lea S* —6C **16**
Lansdowne Rd. *Lea S* —6C **16**
Lansdowne St. *Lea S* —6C **16**
Larch Clo. *S Avon* —5A **6**
Larch Gro. *Warw* —6E **15**
Launce Gro. *H'cte* —1B **28**
Lawford Rd. *Lea S* —4D **22**
Lawson Av. *Tidd* —5E **7**
Lay Gdns. *Rad S* —4G **23**
Lea Clo. *S Avon* —5D **4**
Lea Ct. *S Avon* —2H **9**
Leamington Spa Art Gallery & Mus. —2B 22
Leam Rd. *Lea S* —2H **21**
Leam St. *Lea S* —2D **22**
Leam Ter. *Lea S* —2C **22**
Leam Ter. E. *Lea S* —1D **22**
Lear Gro. *H'cte* —5A **22**
Ledbrook Rd. *Lea S* —2F **17**
Ledbury Rd. *Lea S* —3E **23**
Lee Clo. *Warw* —5C **14**
Leek Wootton. —1D 14
Lee Rd. *Lea S* —2A **22**
Lees, The. *Bis T* —4H **27**
Leicester Ct. *Lea S* —6D **16**
Leicester La. *Lea S* —2C **16**
Leicester St. *Lea S* —6C **16**
Leighton Clo. *Lea S* —3E **17**
Lewis Rd. *Rad S* —5G **23**
Leyburn Clo. *Warw* —6C **14**
Leycester Pl. *Warw* —3C **20**
Leyfields Cres. *Warw* —5B **20**
Lilac Gro. *Warw* —6E **15**
Lillington. —4E 17
Lillington Av. *Lea S* —5B **16**
Lillington Clo. *Lea S* —4C **16**
Lillington Rd. *Lea S* —5C **16**
Lime Av. *Lea S* —3C **16**
Limes Av. *S Avon* —2F **9**
Limes, The. *S Avon* —4A **2**
Lincoln Clo. *Warw* —6C **14**
Linden Clo. *Warw* —5C **14**
Linen St. *Warw* —3B **20**
Linkway. *Lea S* —3A **22**
Lisle Gdns. *Bis T* —4A **28**
Littleworth. —5B 18
Livery St. *Lea S* —1B **22**
Llewellyn Rd. *Lea S* —3C **22**
Lloyd Clo. *H Mag* —3F **19**
Lock Clo. *S Avon* —2E **3**
Lockheed Clo. *Lea S* —4B **22**
Lock La. *Warw* —1B **20**
Lodge Cres. *Warw* —5B **20**
Lodge Rd. *S Avon* —6F **5**
Longbridge. —1H 25
Longfellow Av. *Warw* —5A **20**
Longfield Rd. *Lea S* —3D **22**
Longleat Gro. *Lea S* —3E **23**
Lonsdale Rd. *Lea S* —3D **16**
Lord Leycester Hospital. —3C 20
Loveday Dri. *Lea S* —5A **16**
Lower Av. *Lea S* —2B **22**
Lwr. Cape. *Warw* —6B **14**
Lower Clopton. —2G 5
Lwr. Friars. *Warw* —4B **20**
Lwr. Leam St. *Lea S* —1D **22**
Lower Norton. —5A 18
Lwr. Villiers St. *Lea S* —6C **16**
Lowes Av. *Warw* —6C **14**
Loxley Rd. *S Avon* —1B **10**
Loxley Way. *Lea S* —5C **16**
Lucy's Mill Houses. *S Avon* —2A **10**
Luddington. —5A 8
Luddington Rd. *S Avon* —4D **8**
Ludford Clo. *S Avon* —5D **4**
Lydstep Gro. *Lea S* —2E **23**
Lyndon Ct. *Lea S* —1A **22**
Lynton Clo. *Warw* —6B **14**
Lynwood Wlk. *Lea S* —3E **23**
Lysander Ct. *S Avon* —1H **9** (5D **2**)
Lyster Clo. *Warw* —1H **19**
Lythall Clo. *Rad S* —4H **23**
Lyttleton Rd. *Warw* —1C **20**

Macbeth App. *H'cte* —5H **21**
Maidenhead Clo. *S Avon* —5A **6**
Maidenhead Rd. *S Avon* —6A **6** (1E **3**)
Main St. *Tidd* —5E **7**

Makepeace Av. *Warw* —6D **14**
Malham Rd. *Warw* —6D **14**
Malins, The. *Warw* —3F **21**
Mallard Clo. *S Avon* —4E **5**
Mallory Dri. *Warw* —2B **20**
Mallory Rd. *Bis T* —4G **27**
Maltings Ct. *S Avon* —1C **2**
Maltings, The. *Lea S* (in two parts) —5B **16**
Maltings, The. *S Avon* —1A **10** (5D **2**)
Mander Gro. *Warw* —5H **19**
Manor Ct. *Lea S* —2B **22**
Manor Dri. *Wilm* —1B **4**
Mnr. Farm Cotts. *Ludd* —5B **8**
Manor Gdns. *S Avon* —2F **9**
Manor Grn. *S Avon* —1C **10**
Manor Rd. *Lea S* —4D **16**
Manor Rd. *S Avon* —1C **10**
Mansell St. *S Avon* —6H **5** (2B **2**)
Mantua. *S Avon* —1F **3**
Maple Gro. *S Avon* —4H **5**
Maple Gro. *Warw* —6E **15**
Maple Rd. *Lea S* —3B **22**
Marcroft Pl. *Lea S* —3F **23**
Mark Antony Dri. *H'cte* —5H **21**
Market Corner. *Lea S* —3B **22**
Market Pl. *Warw* —3C **20**
Market St. *Warw* —3B **20**
Markham Dri. *W'nsh* —6D **22**
Marks M. *Warw* —3C **20**
Marlborough Dri. *Syd* —3F **23**
Marloes Wlk. *Syd* —3E **23**
Marsham Clo. *Warw* —1F **21**
Marston Clo. *Lea S* —5D **16**
Marten Clo. *H Mag* —2G **19**
Martin Clo. *S Avon* —4A **6**
Masefield Av. *Warw* —5A **20**
Masefield Rd. *S Avon* —2B **10**
Mason Av. *Lea S* —4D **16**
Masons Ct. *S Avon* —5B **2**
Masons Rd. *S Avon* —5F **5**
Masons Rd. Ind. Est. *S Avon* —5F **5**
Masons Way. *S Avon* —5F **5**
Masters Rd. *Lea S* —4C **22**
Mathecroft. *Lea S* —4E **23**
Matthews Clo. *S Avon* —5A **6**
Maxstoke Gdns. *Lea S* —3B **22**
Maybird Cen. *S Avon* —5H **5**
Maybrook Ind. Est. *S Avon* —5H **5**
Maybrook Rd. *S Avon* —5H **5**
Mayfield Av. *S Avon* —5A **6**
Mayfield Clo. *Lea S* —3E **23**
Mayfield Ct. *S Avon* —6A **6**
Maynard Av. *Warw* —2E **21**
Mayne Clo. *H Mag* —3F **19**
Meadow Clo. *Lea S* —3E **17**
Meadow Clo. *S Avon* —6F **5**
Meadow Lea. *S Avon* —6F **5**
Meadow Rd. *Warw* —2E **21**
Meadows, The. *Leek W* —1E **15**
Mdw. Sweet Rd. *S Avon* —4G **5**
Medley Gro. *W'nsh* —6B **22**
Meer St. *S Avon* —6H **5** (3C **2**)
Melton Rd. *Lea S* —3D **16**
Mercia Way. *Warw* —2F **21**
Mews Rd. *Lea S* —1H **21**
Mickleton Dri. *Hatt P* —5E **13**
Middle Lock La. *Hatt P* —5D **12**
Middle Rd. *Ches* —4H **29**
Milcote Rd. *W Avon* —6D **8**
Mildmay Clo. *S Avon* —2F **9**
Milestone Rd. *S Avon* —3D **10**
Millbank. *Warw* —6E **15**
Millers Rd. *Warw* —1B **20**
Mill Ho. Clo. *Lea S* —1G **21**
Mill Ho. Dri. *Lea S* —1G **21**
Mill Ho. Ter. *Lea S* —1G **21**
Mill La. *Barf* —5H **25**
Mill La. *Cubb* —2H **17**
Mill La. *S Avon* —2A **10**
Mill Rd. *Lea S* —1C **22**
Mill St. *Lea S* —2C **22**
Mill St. *Warw* —3D **20**
Millway Dri. *Bis T* —3A **28**
Milton Av. *Warw* —4A **20**
Milverton. —1A 22
Milverton Ct. *Lea S* —1A **22**
Milverton Cres. *Lea S* —6A **16**
Milverton Cres. W. *Lea S* —6A **16**
Milverton Hill. *Lea S* —1A **22**
Milverton Ter. *Lea S* —1A **22**
Minories, The. *S Avon* —6H **5** (3C **2**)
Minshills Ct. *S Avon* —1D **2**
Minster Clo. *H Mag* —3F **19**
Miranda Dri. *H'cte* —6A **22**
Moat Grn. *Sher* —2G **25**
Mollington Gro. *Hatt P* —5D **12**
Mollington Rd. *W'nsh* —6C **22**
Moncrieff Dri. *Lea S* —4E **23**
Monks Way. *Warw* —3B **20**
Montague Rd. *Warw* —6E **15**
Montgomery Av. *H Hill* —3E **19**
Montgomery Clo. *Shot* —2G **9**
Montgomery Rd. *W'nsh* —5B **22**
Montrose Av. *Lea S* —3C **16**
Monument Way. *S Avon* —4A **6**
Moore Clo. *Warw* —5C **14**
Moore Wlk. *Warw* —2G **21**
Moorhill Rd. *W'nsh* —6C **22**
Moorings, The. *Lea S* —2H **21**
Moreton Clo. *S Avon* —1D **10**
Morrell St. *Lea S* —6B **16**
Morris Dri. *W'nsh* —1D **28**
Morse Rd. *W'nsh* —6D **22**
Morton Ct. *S Avon* —1F **3**
Morton St. *Lea S* —6B **16**
Mosspaul Clo. *Lea S* —5H **15**
Moss St. *Lea S* —2C **22**
Mountbatten Clo. *S Avon* —2F **9**
Mount Cres. *S Avon* —6E **5**
Mt. Pleasant. *S Avon* —6E **5**
Mulberry Clo. *Lea S* —5C **16**
Mulberry Ct. *S Avon* —6A **6** (1D **2**)
Mulberry Dri. *Warw* —1D **20**
Mulberry St. *S Avon* —6A **6** (1D **2**)
Mulberry Tree Shop. Cen., The. *S Avon* —3F **3**
Mullard Dri. *W'nsh* —6D **22**
Murcott Ct. *W'nsh* —6C **22**
Murcott Rd. *W'nsh* —6C **22** (in two parts)
Murcott Rd. E. *W'nsh* —6D **22**
Myton. —3F 21
Myton Cres. *Warw* —3F **21**
Myton Crofts. *Lea S* —2H **21**
Myton Gdns. *Warw* —3E **21**
Myton La. *Warw* —3F **21**
Myton Rd. *Warw & Lea S* —3E **21**

Napton Dri. *Lea S* —5C **16**
Narborough Ct. *Lea S* —1H **21**
Narrow La. *S Avon* —2H **9**
Nashes, The. *Cliff C* —6G **9**
Nash's House. —1A 10 (5D 2)
Neilston St. *Lea S* —2C **22**
Nelson Av. *Warw* —1E **21**
Nelson La. *Warw* —1D **20**
Nevill Clo. *Lea S* —3B **22**
Neville Gro. *Warw* —6D **14**
Newbold Comyn Country Pk. —1E 23
Newbold Pl. *Lea S* —1B **22**
Newbold St. *Lea S* —1C **22**
Newbold Ter. *Lea S* —1B **22**
Newbold Ter. E. *Lea S* —1C **22**
New Broad St. *S Avon* —2H **9**
New Brook St. *Lea S* —1A **22**
Newburgh Cres. *Warw* —1C **20**
Newbury Clo. *Lea S* —3F **23**
New Clo. *H Mag* —3F **19**
New Cotts. *S Avon* —1G **9**
Newdigate. *Lea S* —4E **23**
Newgale Wlk. *Lea S* —2E **23**
Newland Rd. *Lea S* —4E **17**
Newmarket Clo. *S Avon* —2G **9**
Newnham Rd. *Lea S* —4D **16**
New Place & Great Garden. —1A 10 (5D 2)
New River Wlk. *Lea S* —1H **21**
New Rd. *N Lin* —6A **18**
Newsholme Clo. *Warw* —6C **14**
New St. *Cubb* —2G **17**
New St. *Lea S* —2C **22**
New St. *S Avon* —2H **9**
New St. *Tidd* —5E **7**
New St. *Warw* —3C **20**
Nicholson Clo. *Warw* —6D **14**
Noble Clo. *Warw* —4B **20**
Norfolk St. *Lea S* —6C **16**
Normanby Meadows. *W'nsh* —1C **28**
Normandy Clo. *H Mag* —2G **19**
North Clo. *Lea S* —2G **17**
Northcote St. *Lea S* —2D **22**
Northgate. *Warw* —2C **20**
Northgate St. *Warw* —2C **20**
Northumberland Rd. *Lea S* —4A **16**
N. Villiers St. *Lea S* —6C **16**
Northway. *Lea S* —3C **22**
Norton Curlieu La. *Lwr N* —3A **18**
Norton Dri. *Warw* —5C **14**
Norton Lindsey. —6A 18
Nunhold Bus. Cen. *Hatt* —1A **18**
Nursery La. *Lea S* —4C **22**

Oak Ct. *H'cte* —1A **28**
Oakfield Ho. *Lea S* —5B **16**
Oakleigh Rd. *S Avon* —4G **5**
Oakley Wood Rd. *Bis T* (in two parts) —6H **27**
Oakridge Rd. *Lea S* —3E **17**
Oak Rd. *Tidd* —6E **7**
Oaks, The. *Lea S* —1H **21**
Oak Tree Clo. *Lea S* —5C **16**
Oakwood Gro. *Warw* —6E **15**
Oberon Clo. *H'cte* —5A **22**
Offa Rd. *Lea S* —3D **22**
Offchurch La. *Rad S* —3H **23**
Offchurch Rd. *Cubb* —2F **17**
Ogmore Rd. *Lea S* —2D **22**
Oken Ct. *Warw* —2B **20**
Oken Rd. *Warw* —1B **20**
Old Budbrooke Rd. *H Mag* —3E **19**
Old Milverton. —4G 15
Old Milverton La. *Lea S* —4G **15**
Old Milverton Rd. *Lea S* —4G **15**
Old Pound. *Warw* —2C **20**

Old Red Lion Ct. *S Avon* —1A **10** (4F **3**)
Old School La. *H Hill* —5E **19**
Old School La. *Wilm* —1A **4**
Old School M. *Lea S* —4D **16**
Old Sq. *Warw* —3C **20**
Old Sq., The. *Shot* —1F **9**
Old Stone Yd. *Lea S* —6A **16**
Old Town. *S Avon* —1H **9**
Old Town M. *Old T* —2H **9**
Old Tramway Wlk. *S Avon* —1B **10** (4G **3**)
(in three parts)
Old Warwick Rd. *Lea S* —2A **22**
Olympus Av. *Tach P* —4H **21**
Onslow Cft. *Lea S* —5B **16**
Ophelia Dri. *H'cte* —5A **22**
Orchard Ct. *Lea S* —5B **16**
Orchard Pl. *Cliff C* —6G **9**
Orchards, The. *Wilm* —1A **4**
Orchard, The. *Warw* —4D **20**
Orchard Way. *S Avon* —1G **9**
Orrian Clo. *S Avon* —4G **5**
Orsino Clo. *H'cte* —1A **28**
Osborne Ct. *W'nsh* —5C **22**
Oswald Rd. *Lea S* —1H **21**
Othello Av. *H'cte* —6B **22**
Overberry Orchard. *Lea S* —4H **27**
Overell Gro. *Lea S* —5H **15**
Overtons Clo. *Rad S* —4H **23**
Oxford Pl. *Lea S* —6B **16**
Oxford Row. *Lea S* —6B **16**
Oxford St. *Lea S* —6B **16**
Oxstalls Cotts. *S Avon* —3D **6**

Packington Pl. *Lea S* —2C **22**
Packmores. —1D 20
Packmore St. *Warw* —1D **20**
Packsaddle Hill. *S Avon* —1E **7**
Packwood Clo. *Lea S* —4E **23**
Paddock La. *S Avon* —2G **9**
Paddock Pl. *S Avon* —2H **9**
Paddocks, The. *Warw* —2D **20**
Padmore Ct. *Lea S* —3D **22**
Padua. *S Avon* —1F **3**
Palmer Ct. *S Avon* —5F **3**
Palmer Rd. *W'nsh* —5D **22**
Pampas Clo. *S Avon* —4G **5**
Parade. *Lea S* —6B **16**
Paradise St. *Warw* —1D **20**
Park Clo. *Wilm* —1A **4**
Park Ct. *S Avon* —5G **5**
Park Dri. *Lea S* —2A **22**
Parkes Ct. *Warw* —2B **20**
Parkes St. *Warw* —2B **20**
Parklands Av. *Lea S* —3E **17**
Park Rd. *Lea S* —3C **16**
Park Rd. *S Avon* —5H **5**
Park Rd. *Warw* —1D **20**
Park St. *Lea S* —6B **16**
Parmiter Ho. *Lea S* —5B **16**
Parr Clo. *Warw* —3H **21**
Parsonage Clo. *Bis T* —4A **28**
Partridge Rd. *S Avon* —4E **5**
Pattens Rd. *Warw* —6E **15**
Payne Clo. *Lea S* —5C **16**
Payton Ct. *S Avon* —2E **3**
Payton St. *S Avon* —6A **6** (2E **3**)
Peacocks, The. *Warw* —1H **25**
Peel Rd. *Warw* —1C **20**
Pembroke Clo. *Warw* —6D **14**
Pendine Ct. *Lea S* —1H **21**
Penfold Clo. *Bis T* —4A **28**
Penns Clo. *Lea S* —2G **17**
Pennystone Clo. *Lea S* —3F **23**
Penrith Clo. *Lea S* —5G **15**
Percy Rd. *Warw* —1C **20**
Percy St. *S Avon* —5A **6**
Percy Ter. *Lea S* —6H **15**
Pheasant Clo. *S Avon* —5E **5**
Phillippes Rd. *Warw* —6D **14**
Pickard St. *Warw* —2E **21**
Piers Clo. *Warw* —1D **20**
Pimlico La. *A'ton* —1F **11**
Pine Clo. *S Avon* —2F **9**
Pine Ct. *Lea S* —4D **16**
Pinehurst. *Cubb* —1G **17**
Plantagent Pk. *H'cte* —6A **22**
Plato Clo. *Tach P* —4H **21**
Pleasant Way. *Lea S* —5C **16**
Plover Clo. *S Avon* —4F **5**
Plymouth Pl. *Lea S* —2C **22**
Poet's Arbour. *S Avon* —5E **3**
Portland Ct. *Lea S* —6B **16**
Portland M. *Lea S* —1B **22**
Portland Pl. E. *Lea S* —1B **22**
Portland Pl. W. *Lea S* —1A **22**
Portland Row. *Lea S* —1A **22**
Portland St. *Lea S* —1B **22**
Portway Clo. *Lea S* —3F **23**
Potterton Works. *Warw* —1G **21**
Pound La. *Lea S* —4C **16**
Powell Clo. *Bis T* —4A **28**
Powers Ct. *Lea S* —6B **16**
Precinct, The. *Warw* —6E **15**
Price Rd. *Lea S* —3G **17**
Primrose Hill. *Warw* —6A **14**
Prince Regent Ct. *Lea S* —3B **22**
Prince's Dri. *Lea S* —1H **21**
Prince's St. *Lea S* —6D **16**
Priory M. *Warw* —2C **20**
Priory Rd. *Warw* —2C **20**
Priory St. *Lea S* —3B **22**
Priory Ter. *Lea S* —2B **22**
Priory Wlk. *Warw* —2D **20**
Private Rd. *Warw* —1H **19**
Prospect Rd. *Lea S* —4D **22**
Prospero Dri. *H'cte* —6A **22**
Puckerings La. *Warw* —3C **20**
Purcell Clo. *Lea S* —1C **22**
Purser Dri. *Warw* —5H **19**
Purton M. *Lea S* —3E **23**

Quail Clo. *B'ton* —5E **5**
Quarry Clo. *Leek W* —1D **14**
Quarry Fields. *Leek W* —1D **14**
Quarry St. *Lea S* —1G **21**
Queen's Ct. *S Avon* —2H **9**
Queen's Pk. *Lea S* —3A **22**
Queens Sq. *Warw* —3B **20**
Queen St. *Cubb* —2F **17**
Queen St. *Lea S* —6C **16**
Queensway. *Lea S* —3A **22**
Queensway Trad. Est. *Lea S* —3A **22**
Quiney's Rd. *S Avon* —1F **9**
Quinton Clo. *Hatt P* —4D **12**

Radbrook Way. *Lea S* —3F **23**
Radcliffe Gdns. *Lea S* —3C **22**
Radford Hall. *Rad S* —3G **23**
Radford Rd. *Lea S* —2C **22**
Radford Semele. —4G 23
Rainsford Clo. *Cliff C* —6H **9**
Ramsey Rd. *Lea S* —2D **22**
Randolph Clo. *Lea S* —3E **23**
Ranelagh St. *Lea S* —3C **22**
Ranelagh Ter. *Lea S* —3B **22**
Range Mdw. Clo. *Lea S* —4G **15**
Ravensdale Av. *Lea S* —5G **15**
Rawlinson Rd. *Lea S* —5D **16**
Rayford Cvn. Pk. *S Avon* —5C **6**
Raynsford Wlk. *Warw* —6B **14**
Reading Ct. *S Avon* —5D **6**
Reardon Ct. *Warw* —6C **14**
Rectory Clo. *W'nsh* —5D **22**
Redcar Clo. *Lea S* —3D **16**
Redland Rd. *Lea S* —4D **22**
Redlands Cres. *S Avon* —6E **5**
Redwing Clo. *S Avon* —4F **5**
Regal Rd. *S Avon* —5H **5**
Regency Arc. *Lea S* —1B **22**
Regency M. *Lea S* —1C **22**
Regent Gro. *Lea S* —1B **22**
Regent Pl. *Lea S* —2C **22**
Regent St. *Lea S* —2C **22**
Regimental Mus. of the Queen's Own Hussars. —3C 20
Regnier Pl. *H'cte* —1B **28**
Remburn Gdns. *Warw* —1D **20**
Richards Gro. *Lea S* —4C **22**
Richardson Clo. *Warw* —6D **14**
Rich Clo. *Warw* —2E **21**
Rideswell Gro. *W'nsh* —2C **28**
Ridgeley Clo. *Warw* —5C **14**
Ridgeway, The. *Warw* —6E **15**
Ridgewood Clo. *Lea S* —6G **15**
Ridgway, The. *Wilm* —2A **4**
Rigby Clo. *H'cte I* —5H **21**
Rinill Gro. *Lea S* —3F **23**
Risdale Clo. *Lea S* —5H **15**
River Clo. *Lea S* —1H **21**
Rivermead Dri. *Tidd* —5E **7**
Riversdale. *Lea S* —1A **22**
Riverside. *S Avon* —5C **6**
Riverside Wlk. *Warw* —3D **20**
Riversleigh Rd. *Lea S* —6G **15**
Robinia Clo. *Lea S* —6D **16**
Robins Gro. *Warw* —5H **19**
Rochford Ct. *Lea S* —2A **22**
Rock Mill La. *Lea S* —6G **15**
Roe Clo. *Warw* —1D **20**
Rogers Way. *Warw* —5H **19**
Romeo Arbour. *H'cte* —6A **22**
Rookes Ct. *S Avon* —1C **2**
Rosefield Pl. *Lea S* —1B **22**
Rosefield St. *Lea S* —1B **22**
Rosefield Wlk. *Lea S* —1B **22**
Rosewood Cres. *Lea S* —5D **16**
Rotherfield Clo. *Lea S* —2D **22**
Rother St. *S Avon* —1H **9** (6B **2**)
Rothwell Rd. *Warw* —6A **14**
Rowan Clo. *S Avon* —4H **5**
Rowan Dri. *Warw* —1D **20**
Rowborough Clo. *Hatt P* —5E **13**
Rowley Cres. *S Avon* —5A **6**
Rowley Rd. *W'nsh* —6C **22**
Roxburgh Cft. *Lea S* —2D **16**
Royal Leamington Spa. —2C 22
Royal Leamington Spa Tourist Info. Cen. —1B 22
Royal Priors Shop. Cen. *Lea S* —1B **22**
RSC Theatre & Collection. —1A 10 (5F 3)
Rugby Rd. *Lea S* —6H **15**
Rugby Rd. *Lea S & W Weth* —2E **17**
Rushbrook Rd. *S Avon* —3C **10**

Rushmore Pl. *Lea S* —2D **22**
Rushmore St. *Lea S* —2D **22**
Russell St. *Lea S* —6B **16**
Russell Ter. *Lea S* —2C **22**
Ryder Clo. *H Mag* —3F **19**
Rye Clo. *S Avon* —4G **5**
Rye Flds. *Bis T* —4H **27**
Ryland Clo. *Lea S* —3E **23**
Ryland Rd. *Barf* —4A **26**
Ryland St. *S Avon* —2H **9**
Rylstone Way. *Warw* —6C **14**
Ryon Hill. *S Avon* —2E **7**

Sackville Clo. *S Avon* —5E **5**
Sadler Clo. *S Avon* —3H **5**
Saffron Mdw. *S Avon* —2H **9**
Saffron Wlk. *S Avon* —2H **9**
St Albans Clo. *Lea S* —5G **15**
St Andrew's Cres. *S Avon* —1G **9**
St Andrew's Rd. *Lea S* —2D **16**
St Ann's Clo. *Lea S* —2E **23**
St Brides Clo. *Lea S* —3E **23**
Saintbury Clo. *S Avon* —2D **10**
St Catherine's Cres. *W'nsh* —6B **22**
St Chads Rd. *Bis T* —4H **27**
St Christopher's Clo. *Warw* —1B **20**
St Davids Clo. *Lea S* —2E **23**
St Ediths Grn. *Warw* —1F **21**
St George's Clo. *S Avon* —5F **5**
St Georges Rd. *Lea S* —3B **22**
St Govans Clo. *Lea S* —3E **23**
St Gregory's Rd. *S Avon* —6A **6** (1G **3**)
St Helens Rd. *Lea S* —4B **22**
St James Mdw. Rd. *Lea S* —5G **15**
St Johns. *Warw* —2D **20**
St John's Clo. *S Avon* —2H **9**
St John's Ct. *S Avon* —2H **9**
St John's Ct. *Warw* —2D **20**
St John's House. —2D 20
St Johns Rd. *Lea S* —3C **22**
St Laurence Av. *Warw* —4B **20**
St Margaret's Rd. *Lea S* —4D **22**
St Mark's La. *Lea S* —6A **16**
St Mark's M. *Lea S* —6A **16**
St Mark's Rd. *Lea S* —6H **15**
St Martin's Clo. *S Avon* —1G **9**
St Marys Clo. *Warw* —1B **20**
St Mary's Cres. *Lea S* —2D **22**
St Mary's Rd. *Lea S* —2D **22**
St Mary's Rd. *S Avon* —5A **6**
St Mary's Ter. *Lea S* —2D **22**
St Michaels Rd. *Warw* —1A **20**
St Nicholas Chu. St. *Warw* —3D **20**
St Nicholas Rd. *Rad S* —4H **23**
St Nicholas Ter. *Rad S* —5G **23**
St Paul's Clo. *Warw* —3B **20**
St Pauls Sq. *Lea S* —6C **16**
St Paul's Ter. *Warw* —3B **20**
St Peter's Rd. *Lea S* —1B **22**
Saltisford. *Warw* —2B **20**
Saltisford Gdns. *Warw* —1B **20**
Sanctus Ct. *S Avon* —2H **9**
Sanctus Dri. *S Avon* —2H **9**
Sanctus Rd. *S Avon* —2G **9**
Sandel Clo. *S Avon* —6G **5**
Sanders Ct. *Warw* —1G **21**
Sandfield Ct. *S Avon* —2H **9**
Sandfield Rd. *S Avon* —2H **9**
Sandown Clo. *Lea S* —3E **17**
Sandpiper Clo. *S Avon* —4F **5**
Sandy La. *B'dwn* —1A **16**
Sandy Way. *Barf* —6A **26**
Sapphire Dri. *Lea S* —4B **22**
Sargeaunt St. *Lea S* —2B **22**
Satchwell Ct. *Lea S* —1B **22**
Satchwell Pl. *Lea S* —2C **22**
Satchwell Wlk. *Lea S* —1B **22**
Saumur Way. *Warw* —3G **21**
Savages Clo. *Bis T* —4B **28**
Saxon Clo. *S Avon* —1B **10**
Saxon Meadows. *Lea S* —5G **15**
Scar Bank. *Warw* —6C **14**
Scholars Ct. *S Avon* —3A **2**
Scholars La. *S Avon* —1H **9** (5B **2**)
School La. *Rad S* —4G **23**
School La. *Tidd* —4E **7**
Scott Rd. *Lea S* —3D **22**
Seekings, The. *W'nsh* —6D **22**
Semele Clo. *Rad S* —4G **23**
Seven Acre Clo. *Bis T* —4H **27**
Severn Clo. *Lea S* —4E **17**
Severn Mdw. Rd. *S Avon* —2H **9**
Sevincott Clo. *S Avon* —5E **5**
Seymour Clo. *H Mag* —3F **19**
Seymour Gro. *Warw* —3H **21**
Seymour Rd. *S Avon* —2F **9**
Shakespeare Av. *Warw* —4A **20**
Shakespeare Cen., The. —2D 2
Shakespeare Ct. *S Avon* —2E **3**
Shakespeare's Birthplace. —3D 2
Shakespeare St. *S Avon* —6A **6** (2C **2**)
Sharpe Clo. *Warw* —1C **20**
Sheepcote Clo. *Lea S* —6C **16**
Sheep St. *S Avon* —1A **10** (5E **3**)
Shelbourne Rd. *S Avon* —5D **4**
Sheldon Gro. *Warw* —6D **14**
Shelley Av. *Warw* —5A **20**
Shelley Rd. *S Avon* —2B **10**
Sherbourne. —3F 25
Sherbourne Ct. *Sher* —2F **25**
Sherbourne Pl. *Lea S* —5C **16**
Sherbourne Ter. *Lea S* —6C **16**
Sherwood Wlk. *Lea S* —3E **17**
Shipston Rd. *S Avon* —5A **10**
Shires Retail Pk., The. *Warw* —3H **21**
Shopping Cen., The. *Lea S* —4D **22**
Shottery. —6E 5
Shottery. *Shot* —1F **9**
Shottery Rd. *S Avon* —1F **9**
Shrieve's Wlk. *S Avon* —1A **10**
Shrieve's Wlk. Shop. Cen. *S Avon* —5F **3**
Shrubland St. *Lea S* —3B **22** (in two parts)
Shuckburgh Gro. *Lea S* —5D **16**
Shylock Gro. *H'cte* —1A **28**
Sidelands Rd. *S Avon* —6E **5**
Silver Birch Gro. *Lea S* —4B **22**
Slade Hill. *H Mag* —2F **19**
Slade Mdw. *Rad S* —4G **23**
Slingates Rd. *S Avon* —5A **6**
Smith St. *Lea S* —2B **22**
Smith St. *Warw* —2C **20**
Smythe Gro. *Warw* —6C **14**
Snitterfield La. *N Lin* —1A **24**
Solway Clo. *Lea S* —3E **23**
Somers Pl. *Lea S* —1A **22**
Southam Rd. *Rad S* —3G **23**
Southborough Ter. *Lea S* —3C **22**
Southbourne Ho. *S Avon* —2F **3**
Southern La. *S Avon* —2A **10**
Southfields. *Lea S* —4C **16**
S. Green Dri. *S Avon* —1E **9**
Southlea Av. *Lea S* —3A **22**
Southlea Clo. *Lea S* —3A **22**
Southorn Ct. *Lea S* —4F **17**
South Ter. *W'nsh* —6C **22**
South Vw. *H Mag* —3G **19**
S. View Rd. *Lea S* —2E **17**
Southway. *Lea S* —4C **22**
Spartan Clo. *Warw* —5A **22**
Spa Vw. *W'nsh* —5D **22**
Spencer Ct. *S Avon* —2G **9**
Spencer St. *Lea S* —2B **22**
Spencer Yd. *Lea S* —2B **22**
Spilsbury Clo. *Lea S* —5A **16**
Spinney Hill. *Warw* —6E **15**
Spinney, The. *Lea S* —6H **15**
Spring La. *Rad S* —4G **23**
Spring Pool. *Warw* —2C **20**
Springwell Rd. *Lea S* —3F **23**
Spruce Gro. *Lea S* —4B **22**
Square St. *Lea S* —6B **16**
Squirhill Pl. *Lea S* —2D **22**
Stamford Gdns. *Lea S* —6A **16**
Standlake M. *Lea S* —3E **23**
Stand St. *Warw* —3B **20**
Stanley Ct. *Lea S* —2E **23**
Stannells Clo. *S Avon* —4E **9**
Stanton Rd. *Lea S* —3E **23**
Stanton Wlk. *Warw* —6B **14**
Starmer Pl. *Hatt* —4A **12**
Station App. *Lea S* —2B **22**
Station Av. *Warw* —2D **20**
Station Rd. *S Avon* —6H **5** (3A **2**)
Station Rd. *Warw* —2D **20**
Station Rd. *Wilm* —1A **4**
Staunton Rd. *Lea S* —4C **22**
Stephenson Clo. *Lea S* —6G **15**
Stidfall Gro. *Lea S* —3F **23**
Stirling Av. *Lea S* —2D **16**
Stockton Gro. *Lea S* —5C **16**
Stonehouse Clo. *Lea S* —2F **17**
Stone Ho. M. *Leek W* —1D **14**
Stoneleigh Rd. *B'dwn* —2B **16**
Stoneway Gro. *Lea S* —3F **23**
Stoney La. *Hatt* —3A **12**
Strachey Av. *Lea S* —5A **16**
Stratford Brass Rubbing Cen. —1A 10
Stratford Butterfly & Jungle Safari. —1B 10 (6H 3)
Stratford Ct. *S Avon* —2C **2**
Stratford Northern By-Pass. *S Avon* —5C **4**
Stratford Rd. *Sher & Warw* —3E **25**
Stratford Rd. *S Avon & H Lucy* —1F **7**

Stratford Shire Horse Cen. —4A 10
Stratford Teddy Bear Mus. —6H 5 (3B 2)
Stratford-upon-Avon. —6A 6 (3E 3)
Stratford-upon-Avon Race Course. —3G 9
Stratford-upon-Avon Tourist Info. Cen. —6A 6 (3G 3)
Strathearn Rd. *Lea S* —6A **16**
Stretton Cres. *Lea S* —4D **22**
Stuart Clo. *Warw* —4B **20**
Stuart Ct. *Lea S* —6A **16**
Styles Clo. *H Mag* —2F **19**
Styles Clo. *Lea S* —2C **22**
Sudbury Clo. *Lea S* —5E **17**
Suffolk St. *Lea S* —6C **16**
Summer Ct. *S Avon* —1E **3**
Summerton Rd. *W'nsh* —6C **22**
Sumner Clo. *H Mag* —3F **19**
Sunshine Cotts. *Shot* —1F **9**
Surrey Ct. *Warw* —1C **20**
Sussex Ct. *Warw* —1C **20**
Sutherland Clo. *Warw* —6C **14**
Swadling St. *Lea S* —3B **22**
Swain Crofts. *Lea S* —3D **22**
Swallow Clo. *S Avon* —4A **6**
Swanfold. *Wilm* —1A **4**
Swans Clo. *Wilm* —1A **4**
Swan's Nest La. *S Avon* —1B **10** (6H **3**)
Swan St. *Lea S* —6C **16**
Swan St. *Warw* —3C **20**
Swan Theatre. —6F 3
Swift Rd. *S Avon* —4A **6**
Sycamore Clo. *S Avon* —4H **5**
Sycamore Gro. *Warw* —6E **15**
Sydenham. —4E 23
Sydenham Dri. *Lea S* —3D **22**
Sydenham Ind. Est. *Lea S* —3D **22**

Tachbrook Ct. *Lea S* —3B **22**
Tachbrook Mallory. —3B 28
Tachbrook Pk. Bus. Cen. *Tach P* —4A **22**
Tachbrook Pk. Dri. *Warw* —3H **21**
Tachbrook Rd. *Lea S* —6B **22**
Tachbrook St. *Lea S* —3C **22**
Talbot Ct. *Lea S* —6C **16**
Talbot Rd. *S Avon* —5A **6**
Tamora Clo. *H'cte* —6H **21**
Tasker's Way. *S Avon* —1A **10** (4D **2**)
Tatnall Gro. *Warw* —1C **20**
Tavern La. *Shot* —1F **9**
Tavistock St. *Lea S* —6B **16**
Taylor Av. *Lea S* —5D **16**
Taylor Ct. *Warw* —2B **20**
Teal Clo. *S Avon* —4E **5**
Telford Av. *Lea S* —2D **16**
Templars, The. *Warw* —4D **20**
Temple Gro. *Warw* —4B **20**
Tennyson Av. *Warw* —5A **20**
Tennyson Rd. *S Avon* —3B **10**
Terrett Ct. *S Avon* —1A **10** (4D **2**)
Terry Av. *Lea S* —6G **15**
Theatre St. *Warw* —3B **20**
Thomas St. *Lea S* —6C **16**
Thornley Clo. *Rad S* —4H **23**
Thorn Stile Clo. *Cubb* —1G **17**
Thornton Clo. *Wood P* —6D **14**
Three Cornered Clo. *Cubb* —1G **17**
Thurmaston Ct. *Lea S* —5B **16**
Thursfield Rd. *Lea S* —4D **16**
Tibbits Ct. *Warw* —3C **20**
Tiddington. —5E 7
Tiddington Ct. *Tidd* —5E **7**
Tiddington Rd. *S Avon* —1B **10**
Tidmarsh Rd. *Leek W* —1E **15**
Tidmington Clo. *Hatt P* —5E **13**
Timon Vw. *H'cte* —6A **22**
Timothy's Bri. Rd. *S Avon* —4F **5**
Timothy's Bri. Rd. Ind. Est. *S Avon* —5F **5**
Tink-A-Tank. *Warw* —3C **20**
Titan Bus. Cen. *Warw* —5A **22**
Tithe Barn Clo. *H Mag* —2F **19**
Toll Ga. Clo. *S Avon* —6D **4**
Tower Clo. *S Avon* —4A **6**
Tower St. *Lea S* —2C **22**
Townesend Clo. *Warw* —6D **14**
Townsend Rd. *Tidd* —6E **7**
Tredington Pk. *Hatt P* —5E **13**
Tressel Cft. *H'cte* —1A **28**
Trevelyan Clo. *S Avon* (in two parts) —5E **5**
Trevelyan Cres. *S Avon* —5E **5**
Trinculo Gro. *H'cte* —1B **28**
Trinity Clo. *Old T* —2A **10**
Trinity College. *S Avon* —6C **2**
Trinity M. *Warw* —2D **20**
Trinity Pl. *S Avon* —1H **9**
Trinity St. *Lea S* —6B **16**
Trinity St. *S Avon* —2H **9**
Trojan Bus. Cen. *Warw* —5A **22**
Troutbeck Av. *Lea S* —5G **15**
Trueman Clo. *Warw* —1C **20**
Tudor Ct. *Warw* —4B **20**
Turner Clo. *Warw* —5H **19**
Turpin Ct. *Lea S* —3B **22**
Twycross Wlk. *Warw* —6B **14**
Tybalt Clo. *H'cte* —5H **21**
Tyler St. *S Avon* —6A **6** (2E **3**)

Ullswater Av. *Lea S* —5G **15**
Union Rd. *Lea S* —6A **16**
Union St. *S Avon* —6A **6** (3E **3**)
Union Wlk. *Lea S* —2C **22**
Upper Billesley. —3A 4
Up. Grove St. *Lea S* —6A **16**
Up. Hill St. *Lea S* —6C **16**
Up. Holly Wlk. *Lea S* —6C **16**
Upper Milcote. —5G 9

Valentine Clo. *S Avon* —2G **9**
Valley Rd. *Lill* —4D **16**
Valley Rd. *Rad S* —5G **23**
Valley, The. *Rad S* —5G **23**
Verden Av. *Warw* —5H **19**
Verdon Pl. *Barf* —5A **26**
Verdun Clo. *W'nsh* —1D **28**
Vermont Gro. *Lea S* —3F **23**
Verney Dri. *S Avon* —4H **5**
Verney Gdns. *S Avon* —4H **5**
Vernon Clo. *Lea S* —4A **16**
Verona. *S Avon* —2F **3**
Vicarage Fld. *Warw* —1F **21**
Vicarage La. *Sher* —2F **25**
Vicarage Ri. *Lea S* —4A **28**
Vicarage Rd. *Lea S* —4D **16**
Victoria Bus. Pk. *Lea S* —2C **22**
Victoria Clo. *S Avon* —6A **6** (1D **2**)
Victoria Colonade. Lea S (off Victoria Ter.) —2B 22
Victoria M. *Warw* —2B **20**
Victoria Rd. *Lea S* —1A **22**
Victoria St. *Lea S* —2A **22**
Victoria St. *Warw* —2B **20**
Victoria Ter. *Lea S* —1B **22**
Villebon Way. *W'nsh* —1C **28**
Villiers St. *Lea S* —6C **16**
Vincent Av. *S Avon* —5H **5**
Vincent St. *Lea S* —6C **16**
Vine La. *Warw* —1C **20**
Viscount Clo. *Lea S* —3B **22**
Vittle Dri. *Warw* —2B **20**

Wackrill Dri. *Lea S* —4E **17**
Wade Gro. *Warw* —5C **14**
Wake Gro. *Warw* —4H **19**
Waldron Ct. *S Avon* —6A **6** (2D **2**)
Walford Gro. *Warw* —6D **14**
Walkers Rd. *S Avon* —4A **6**
Wallace Ct. *Warw* —2B **20**
Waller St. *Lea S* —5C **16**
Waller Way. *W'nsh* —1C **28**
Wallwin Ct. *Warw* —3B **20**
Walnut Dri. *Lea S* —4D **16**
Ward Gro. *Warw* —2G **21**
Ward's Hill. *N Lin* —6A **18**
Warmington Gro. *Warw* —1H **19**
Warneford M. *Lea S* —2C **22**
Warner Clo. *Warw* —6B **14**
Warren Clo. *Lea S* —4B **16**
Warwick. —3C 20
Warwick By-Pass. *Barf* —2D **26**
Warwick By-Pass. *Warw* —4G **19**
Warwick Castle. —3C 20
Warwick Ct. *Lea S* —6B **16**
Warwick Ct. *S Avon* —6A **6** (1F **3**) (in two parts)
Warwick Cres. *S Avon* —6B **6** (1H **3**)
Warwick Doll Mus. —3C 20
Warwick Ho. *S Avon* —1C **2**
Warwick New Rd. *Lea S* —1G **21**
Warwick Pl. *Lea S* —1H **21**
Warwick Race Course. —3A 20
Warwick Rd. *B Hill & Sher* —6B **24**
Warwick Rd. *Leek W & Ken* —1D **14**
Warwick Rd. *S Avon* —6A **6** (3F **3**)
Warwickshire Mus. —3C 20
Warwickshire Yeomanry Mus. —3C 20
Warwicks, The. *H Mag* —3F **19**
Warwick St. *Lea S* —6A **16**
Warwick Technology Pk. *Warw* —4F **21**
Warwick Ter. *Lea S* —6A **16**
Warwick Tourist Info. Cen. —3C 20
Wasdale Clo. *Lea S* —6H **15**
Washbourne Rd. *W'nsh* —6C **22**
Wasperton La. *Barf* —6A **26**
Waterloo Ct. *Warw* —1E **21**
Waterloo Dri. *S Avon* —2D **10**
Waterloo Pl. *Lea S* —6B **16**
Waterloo Ri. *S Avon* —3D **10**
Waterloo St. *Lea S* —2D **22**
Watersfield Gdns. *Lea S* —2E **23**
Waterside. *S Avon* —1A **10** (6E **3**)
Watery La. *Sher* —2G **25**
Wathen Rd. *Lea S* —5C **16**
Wathen Rd. *Warw* —1C **20**
Watson Clo. *Warw* —6C **14**
Waverley Rd. *Lea S* —3C **22**
Waverton M. *Lea S* —3E **23**

Wavy Tree Clo. *Warw* —2B **20**
Weale Gro. *Warw* —6D **14**
Wedgnock Grn. *Warw* —1B **20**
Wedgnock Ind. Est. *Warw* —6H **13**
Wedgnock La. *Beau* —1E **13** (in two parts)
Wedgnock La. *Warw* —1A **20**
Weilerswist Dri. *W'nsh* —5B **22**
Welcombe Cotts. *S Avon* —5A **6**
Welcombe Hills Obelisk. —2B 6
Welcombe Hills Viewpoint. —2B 6
Welcombe Rd. *S Avon* —6A **6** (1G **3**)
Welford Gro. *Hatt P* —4D **12**
Wellesbourne Gro. *S Avon* —1H **9** (4A **2**)
Wellesbourne Rd. *A'ton* —4F **7**
Wellesbourne Rd. *Barf* —5H **25**
Wellington Rd. *Lea S* —4D **16**
Welsh Clo. *Warw* —5C **14**
Welsh Rd. *Cubb & Off* —4H **17**
Welton Rd. *Warw* —6B **14**
Wentworth Rd. *Lea S* —3F **23**
Westbury Ct. *Warw* —2E **21**
Westcliff Dri. *Warw* —5C **14**
Western Rd. *S Avon* —6H **5** (1A **2**)
Western Rd. Ind. Est. *S Avon* —6H **5** (1A **2**)
Westfield Clo. *S Avon* —4H **5**
Westgate Clo. *Warw* —3B **20**
Westgate Ho. *Warw* —3C **20**
W. Green Dri. *S Avon* —6D **4**
Westgrove Ter. *Lea S* —1H **21**
Westham La. *Barf* —6G **25**
Westhill Rd. *B'dwn* —1C **16**
Westlea Rd. *Lea S* —3A **22**
Weston Clo. *Lea S* —3E **23**
Weston Ct. *Warw* —2D **20**
West St. *Lea S* —2C **22**
West St. *S Avon* —2H **9** (6C **2**)
West St. *Warw* —4B **20**
W. View Rd. *Lea S* —2E **17**
Wharf Rd. *Avon I* —5H **5**
Wharf St. *Warw* —2E **21**
Wheathill Clo. *Lea S* —5A **16**
Whiteacre Rd. *Lea S* —5C **16**
Whiteheads Ct. *Lea S* —6B **16**
Whitethorn Dri. *Lea S* —5D **16**
Whitfield Clo. *Tidd* —5E **7**
Whitmore Rd. *W'nsh* —6C **22**
Whitnash. —5C 22
Whitnash Rd. *W'nsh* —5D **22**
Whittington Clo. *Warw* —1F **21**
Wickham Ct. *Lea S* —3D **16**
Wilkins Clo. *Barf* —5H **25**
Willes Rd. *Lea S* —6C **16**
Willes Ter. *Lea S* —1D **22**
Williams Rd. *Rad S* —5G **23**
William St. *Lea S* —1C **22**
William Tarver Clo. *Warw* —2E **21**
Willow Clo. *W'nsh* —1D **28**
Willow Ct. *H'cte* —1A **28**
Willow Sheets Mdw. *Cubb* —1G **17**
Willows N., The. *S Avon* —6G **5**
Willows, The. *S Avon* —1G **9**
Wilmcote. —1A 4
Wilnecote Gro. *Lea S* —4D **22**
Wincott Clo. *S Avon* —2C **10**
Windermere Dri. *Lea S* —5H **15**
Winderton Av. *Hatt* —5D **12**
Windmill Cft. *Lea S* —2F **17**
Windmill Hill. *Lea S* —2F **17**
Windmill Rd. *Lea S* —4B **22**
Windsor Ct. *Lea S* —1B **22**
Windsor Ct. *S Avon* —6H **5** (3C **2**)
Windsor Pl. *Lea S* —1B **22**
Windsor St. *Lea S* —1B **22**
Windsor St. *S Avon* —6H **5** (3C **2**)
Winslow Clo. *Lea S* —6G **15**
Winston Clo. *S Avon* —2F **9**
Winston Cres. *Lea S* —4E **17**
Wise Gro. *Warw* —5C **14**
Wise St. *Lea S* —2B **22**
Wise Ter. *Lea S* —2B **22**
Woburn Clo. *Syd* —3F **23**
Woodbine Cotts. *Lea S* —1A **22**
Woodbine St. *Lea S* —1A **22**
Woodcote Dri. *Leek W* —1D **14**
Woodcote La. *Leek W* —1D **14**
Woodcote Rd. *Lea S* —4A **16**
Woodcote Rd. *Warw* —1D **20**
Woodhouse St. *Warw* —3B **20**
Woodland Rd. *S Avon* —4H **5**
Woodloes Av. N. *Warw* —6C **14**
Woodloes Av. S. *Warw* —6C **14**
Woodloes La. *Guys C* —4C **14**
Woodloes Park. —5B 14
Woodman Ct. *S Avon* —5H **5**
Wood St. *Lea S* —1C **22**
Wood St. *S Avon* —6H **5** (4D **2**)
Woodville Rd. *Warw* —1C **20**
Woodward Clo. *W'nsh* —1C **28**
Woodway. *H Mag* —1E **19**
Woodway Av. *H Mag* —3F **19**
Wooton Ct. *Lea S* —5B **16**
Wootton Clo. *S Avon* —1D **10**
Wordsworth Av. *Warw* —4B **20**
World of Shakespeare. —4F 3
Wychwood Clo. *Bis T* —4A **28**
Wye Clo. *Lea S* —4E **17**

Yardley Clo. *Warw* —5D **14**
Yarranton Clo. *S Avon* —4G **5**
Yeomanry Clo. *Warw* —2D **20**
Yew Tree Ct. *Lea S* —4B **22**
York Rd. *Lea S* —1B **22**
York Wlk. *Lea S* —1B **22**
Young Clo. *Warw* —4H **19**

Food for the Journey

Numbers
Christopher Wright with Elizabeth McQuoid
978 1 78359 720 8

Revelation 1 – 3
Paul Mallard with Elizabeth McQuoid
978 1 78359 712 3

Romans 5 - 8
John Stott with Elizabeth McQuoid
978 1 78359 718 5

Ruth
Alistair Begg with Elizabeth McQuoid
978 1 78359 525 9

Praise for the series

'This devotional series is biblically rich, theologically deep and full of wisdom . . . I recommend it highly.' **Becky Manley Pippert, speaker, author of *Out of the Saltshaker and into the World* and creator of the Live/Grow/ Know course and series of books**

'These devotional guides are excellent tools.' **John Risbridger, Minister and Team Leader, Above Bar Church, Southampton**

'These bite-sized banquets . . . reveal our loving Father weaving the loose and messy ends of our everyday lives into his beautiful, eternal purposes in Christ.' **Derek Burnside, Principal, Capernwray Bible School**

'I would highly recommend this series of 30-day devotional books to anyone seeking a tool that will help [him or her] to gain a greater love of Scripture, or just simply . . . to do something out of devotion. Whatever your motivation, these little books are a must-read.' **Claud Jackson, *Youthwork* Magazine**

Available from your local Christian bookshop or **www.ivpbooks.com**

Food for the Journey THEMES

The **Food for the Journey: Themes** series offers offers daily devotions from much loved Bible teachers at the Keswick Convention, exploring how particular themes are woven through the Bible and what we can learn from them today. In a convenient, pocket-sized format, these little books are ideal to accompany you wherever you go.

Available in the series

Joy
978 1 78974 163 6
'A rich feast!'
Edrie Mallard

Persevere
978 1 78974 102 5
'Full of essential theology.'
Catherine Campbell

Pray
978 1 78974 169 8
'The ideal reboot.'
Julian Hardyman

The Cross
978 1 78974 191 9
'A must-read.'
Gavin Calver

Confident
978 1 78974 190 2
'A beautiful collection.'
Elinor Magowan

Available from your local Christian bookshop or **www.ivpbooks.com**